SOLO TRAVEL

Try it at least once. . .

Diary of a Traveling Black Women: A Guide to International Travel

Mini Travel Guide Series:

Dubai, Abu Dhabi & The 5 Other Emirates You Didn't Know About...

Jamaica: Likkle, but Tallawah!

Studying Abroad for Black Women

Iceland: Nature, Nurture, & Adventure

Solo Travel: Try It At Least Once!

and more...

Diary of a Traveling Black Woman:
A Guide to International Travel

"Mini Travel Guide Series"
Volume V - Solo Travel

Solo Travel:
Try it at least once...

Marilene Shane

Grace Royal International, LLC
Atlanta, GA

Cover Model: Marilene Shane
Cover Design: Nadine C. Duncan
Interior Design: Nadine C. Duncan

ISBN: 9781099172250

1st Edition, August 2019
Travel Guide Series, Volume V
Printed in the United States of America

Published in the United States by:
Traveling Black Women™
Grace Royal International, LLC
Atlanta, GA 30316

www.travelingblackwomen.com

This travel guide is dedicated to my parents, Michael and Jeanette Shane, the people who encouraged me to chase the horizon in every area of my life. Because of you, I am unafraid to stretch my limits. Thank you for pushing my boat away from the shore.

Contents

#TRAVELINGBLACKWOMEN

" *Traveling alone can be the scariest, most liberating, life changing experience of your life. Try it at least once.*"
-*Anonymous*

Preface

The world is much smaller than we were taught to believe. These days, traveling to the other side of the world is doable for everyone, and the booming black travel movement is being led by black women. We are seeing things we once only read about in books, and bringing others with us... sometimes kicking and screaming.

I am an avid traveler, traveling internationally many times a year. While I enjoy the traditional group trip, I LIVE for what I call "Solo Missions." These are the trips where my company is the only one that I value, and I am completely in control of what I do. The itinerary is flexible and everything is completely up to me. Such an amazing feeling!

As you can imagine, the questions from friends and family soon come. People ask me why I solo travel so much. I simply ask them why they don't. Solo Missions allow me to come home to myself every time I embark on one. Is it for everyone? No. But should everyone try it at least once? A resounding "YES!"

Be it venturing off the beaten path to recharge and recalibrate in Zanzibar, kick it in Barcelona, connect with the culture in

Kenya, or detox from the world in Bali, you will regain or find a piece of yourself with every adventure.

Everyone has it in them to travel the world solo. It's one of those things you must throw caution to the wind and do. To date (August 2019), I've traveled to 25 countries. In the past 4 years, 11 of these trips have been solo.

Don't get me wrong, I enjoy creating new memories with family and friends through travel, but I believe that the most growth and fulfillment I've found is when I've been completely on my own, and responsible for everything from choosing locations to itinerary planning.

You may wonder why a 44-year-old Black Woman from Michigan is writing a travel guide on solo travel. What makes me knowledgeable on the topic? Well, five years ago I packed my bags and embarked on the ultimate solo mission--relocating to Abu Dhabi for work. I didn't know a soul and was leaving home for the first time. Yet despite it all, it was the best decision of my life.

In the U.S. I was an established educator and principal of an elementary school. I could have very easily stayed in that comfort zone. But, there has always been a desire in me to see the world, experience new cultures, and stretch myself in every way.

We, as Black women, are known for stepping outside of the boundaries others have created for us and charting our own course. This drive to do something outside of our comfort zones is what will make your solo mission amazing.
I'm assuming that this same drive is within you. You've picked up this guide because you've considered "getting lost" on a solo

mission in an amazing locale. Deep inside you feel that you are ready to take the step into the unknown, release fears, and have an awesome travel experience. I'm super excited for you because once you venture out there solo, you won't return the same.

I'll share some important tips about solo missions; like what to consider when selecting a destination, determining your trip's purpose, the financial aspects, and personal safety.

I'll also touch on that inevitable question of loneliness. If you haven't already asked yourself, someone else will undoubtedly ask you about it when you tell them you are going out on your own.

It is my hope that this guide will help you create an unforgettable experience that will get you addicted to traveling solo. Getting lost (safely, of course) in the world alone is one of the best things you can ever do. It opens doors and empowers at the same time.

It's very rewarding, trust me.

Your Purpose

"*Travel far enough, you meet yourself.*" *Anonymous*

Our comfort zones house the safest versions of ourselves. The decision to step out of that space and see what you are made of through the natural human inclination to wander is monumental and must be done with intention. Some even call it 'mindful travel.' Something has sparked that drive in you, and it calls for a moment of reflection to figure out the 'why' before you can figure out the 'where.'

If you take the time to understand your motivations it will help with all the subsequent decisions that will make your first solo trip outstanding. Let me congratulate you, you've made the biggest decision you'll need to make: You are officially going on a 'Solo Mission'. Well done! Trust me, that first step is the hardest, but now you're ready to get the ball rolling.

The initial question you must ask yourself when thinking of where you want to go is *why* you want to go. Some solo trips are about relaxing and taking each day as it comes, while others are about challenging yourself. Something led you to decide that a solo trip was needed, get in touch with that feeling.

When I traveled to Rio, Brazil I faced fears and literally jumped off a mountain with a kite on my back. Hands down the most dangerous and exhilarating thing I've ever physically done! That trip was centered around facing fears and stepping outside of my comfort zone. My entire life I'd convinced myself that I had a fear of heights, but I found a strength I didn't realize I had. After the experience of hang gliding on that trip, I don't pass up anything too daring when I travel. This is because I was open to new things and knew the reason for the trip before I left home. I believe it is important to have a purpose, even if it's simply the experience of traveling alone.

Starting Small. . .

Solo travel is chalk full of decisions, but you'll find that once you make the first one, the remaining will seem to flow easily. What are the financial costs? Is it safe to travel as a woman where I am considering? How will a Black Woman be received where I go? What kinds of activities are there to do there?

For some of us, taking baby steps into solo travel is the best direction to take. Consider starting with some place close to where you live, where the people speak the same language and it isn't too far from what you are used to. The purpose is just to try some time setting things up and going off on your own to get a "feel" for what it will be like when you do take a longer and farther trip.

Easing into solo travel is a good idea if you are hesitant about it. This approach worked out perfectly for me and gave me the confidence to later try places that had fewer infrastructures in place.

As a Black Woman traveling by herself, your safety and budget are top things to consider. We are most often taking care of our families, working long hours, and trying to maintain some type of social life with the little time left in the day. This is your time to put yourself first. Choosing a destination that is aligned with your immediate need for self-care is critical. If you feel safe and your money goes farther, you can create an amazing trip!

Your Top 5!

I encourage you to think about where you've always wanted to go and list the top five destinations. Research a bit to see which of those locations lend themselves more to group activities, like partying in Cabo or going to Carnival in Trinidad. Those will quickly drop off your list to be saved for a time when you can go with others. Also consider weather trends, available excursions, transportation and lodging expenses. Narrow down your list by scratching off the places that don't match your immediate needs.

Nine times out of ten your purpose for traveling will determine your destination. When I first began traveling on my own, my travel list included places I'd heard were solo travel friendly. My initial 'Solo Mission Top 5' included Barcelona, Budapest, Bangkok, Bali, and Zanzibar. I decided that I wanted my first trip to be a place that felt somewhat like what I was used to at home in the States. This would allow me to operate as I would back home in Houston, and it would be a gradual release into solo travel.

I decided on Barcelona, Spain for my first solo mission and had the most amazing time. Reflecting back, Barcelona was great, but it was somewhat expensive. In hindsight, I would encourage first time solo travelers to consider destinations in

Southeast Asia like Thailand, Bali, or Malaysia, as they are not only budget-friendly, but also very safe and easy to navigate on your own.

The great thing about deciding where to go on a solo mission is that only your voice counts! You can literally end up any-where! I find that what is happening in my life typically guides my destination decisions. For example, whenever I recognize that I need to relax, I immediately think of a destination that includes beaches, slow days, and massages at the spa. When I traveled to Zanzibar, Tanzania, I needed a relaxing holiday full of beach days and fruity drinks. Work was a bit stressful at the time and I needed not to think for a few days. Zanzibar was perfect.

The Experience. .

Again, decide what environment you feel like experiencing. Would the hustle and bustle of a city match your vibe, or do you want to connect with nature? Do you need an escape from your current reality in the hills detoxing or to be active and adventurous? Maybe the goal of your solo excursion is to fully immerse yourself in the culture of the destination, or simply to indulge in the freedom of being completely uninhibited by others' thoughts or ideas about a location.

Being completely in charge of what is to come each day is what I value most about traveling by myself. I enjoy fully getting in-volved with the life of the location without worrying that my companions may be bored with the itinerary or that contrary personalities may begin to come through. In many ways, being alone grants a sense of freedom that we don't usually find in our every day lives. Embrace it.

As I reflect on the trips I've taken on my own, I've always considered the impact the destination has made historically, especially regarding black people, and why it is on my "lived list" at all. For example, knowing the history of Zanzibar, Tanzania and my personal connection to Africa as a Black Woman, I didn't want to completely miss out on touring the island and learning more. When I traveled there solo, I decided that I would set aside one day to tour and learn about the place, but the other four days would be spent with absolutely no itinerary--just taking each day as it came. That's the beauty of the solo trip! You can do everything or nothing depending only on how *you* are feeling.

Yoga/Detox Retreats

While we are discussing purposeful trips, it is always good to have a grasp on what you need from your solo mission. One type of trip that is getting more and more popular with female solo travelers are yoga/detox retreats. As more of us make a conscience effort to take care of our health, you will see people of all ages eating better and exercising to maintain their health. A great way to reinforce this healthy lifestyle while still traveling and having fun is going to an all-inclusive health retreat. These retreats will most often include sunrise and sunset yoga, other exercise activities (some even have surfing!), meditation, hiking, daily spa treatments and massages, healthy food options like vegan and vegetarian menus, and opportunities to relax.

I mention this to stress the point I was making earlier about knowing why you're making the decision to travel solo before deciding on where. If you want to kick start weight loss, detox from the world and the foods you've been consuming or just reclaim peace, the possibilities are endless. Once you decide this type of trip is what you'd like to do, you can search for retreats that have the itineraries that meet your desired outcomes.

Southeast Asia and Central America (to name a few) have many retreats that are very affordable. It's also important to note that there are some health retreats owned and operated by Black Women that cater to women of color within their packages. The goal is to practice mindfulness, do some self-care, and focus on emotional well-being.

As with every solo trip you plan to embark on, do your homework, read reviews, and research if the retreat is a match for you.

Solo Travel Locations

For first time solo travelers there are a number of places that really lend themselves to solo travel. Great solo travel locations are easy to navigate and have warm and helpful locals. The cost of living is also low and meeting other Black travelers is relatively easy. For first time solo travelers, you can opt to choose a destination where the language and customs are similar to those you already know. If you aren't one to ease slowly into solo adventures, destinations abroad with a group may be where you begin, and you can branch out from there.

Of the eleven locations I've traveled solo, the easiest to travel around were Bangkok and Phuket, Thailand; Zanzibar, Tanzania; Bali, Indonesia; Paris, France; and Barcelona, Spain. To be honest, Paris and Barcelona were more expensive than the other locations, but they provided me with a different type of solo experience that I genuinely loved.

At the end of the day your purpose for traveling solo will direct your decision. The great thing to remember is that most places are actually solo friendly. If you know why you want to go off on your own, the map will lead you to the best place to find what you need.

Trust your instincts and be patient with yourself, the right location will come!

The

Planning

Process

"...*Experiences are Currency.*"

*S*o you've settled on a destination... Well done! I find that following a step by step process for considering the financial aspects of travel has helped me find great deals and taken some of the pressure off this part of the planning:

1. Select your destination. Review travel visa requirements and general safety advisories for the location you are contemplating. A great place to do this is VisaHQ.com. You can check visa requirements for any destination on this site.

2. Research flights and hotel specials, typically using travel booking sites that may bundle costs for good deals. Be flexible with your schedule for deals on tickets and hotel accommodations. You'll find leaving one day earlier or later can be the difference between paying a lot or a little on flights, (which is where the bulk of your money may be spent when traveling). You may also find that being open to traveling midweek may garner great results on deals with some airline carriers.

3. Research the lodging options you find to ensure

they have all the amenities and a good physical location that meet your expectations when traveling.

4. *Research* the top 10 things to do there. I always create a list of "Must Dos" that guide the creation of my itinerary. Since I consider myself a foodie, looking for local spots to eat before I travel are included on a 'Must Eats' list. Many online Black travel groups have recommendations from fellow travelers for things that can't be missed all over the world. I rely on the connections that I've made in these groups because there are a lot of solo travelers, especially women, who have insights into what a black woman should experience when on these kinds of trips. That perspective is key, because they sit in your shoes! I can't stress enough how important it is to research before you go. TripAdvisor is a go-to of mine for the best things to do in every city, with reviews shared by other travelers. It isn't the only place to find activities of interest to you, there are mobile apps such as Viator, which gives a full list of activities in any given city in the world and the option to purchase tickets for them should you see something that is on your "Must Do" list.

5. *Consider* transportation costs, connect with local guides and research public transport there based upon possible itinerary choices. Traveling can be expensive for anyone, whether in a group or on your own. The key is to find small ways to lessen costs and still have the enjoyable experience you envisioned at the onset of your planning. At the start of every solo trip, I assess how much I have in my travel budget and see if that amount matches the trip I've crafted in my head. If the two match, it's full steam ahead.

You will begin your solo mission planning like any other trip, but this time with the additional reminder that you are the only person who will be responsible for paying, there is no splitting of costs. Assess what's important to you as a traveler. Do you want a five-star hotel or all-inclusive resort? Maybe you want to spend more money on activities at your destination and can go for less expensive amenities in hotel selection. My overall travel budget list includes these things: cost of transportation in air and on land, lodging, excursions/activities, entertainment, eating, and souvenir shopping. When I first began traveling a lot, I utilized Expedia often and soon reached Gold status, which provides certain perks such as VIP status at hotels. When you book a hotel using the website or mobile app, you get offers such as room upgrades upon check-in or discounts on food and beverages throughout the length of your stay. These "extras" add to the overall travel experience and help you save on overhead. There's nothing like getting to your hotel to check in and hearing those magical words, "You are VIP, we have upgraded your room for free!" It feels like winning the lottery. When I traveled to Zanzibar, Tanzania, my room was upgraded to a suite on the top floor of the hotel. It was amazing and sold me on using travel apps or travel based search engines to book for as much as I can. I highly encourage use of "book it yourself" travel sites, as there are many out there that help alleviate costs. I use Booking.com often, where you can also earn 'Genius' status, which gives discounts on final hotel room costs. The key is to compare the prices you are quoted from sites to decide which one to use. We all want to save money!

As with any meaningful journey, going off on your own may

require more from you financially than you'd care to give, but you do what you must in order to enjoy the best experiences traveling has to offer.

Single Supplements...

Remember when I told you that when traveling solo it's only you responsible for 100% of the financial costs? There is no better example of this than when dealing with single supplements. When booking tours, hotel rooms and cruises you may incur charges for traveling by yourself instead of in a pair. These charges are called "single supplements," which is the charge solo travelers have to pay for traveling alone, because most hotel rooms and ship cabins are built under the assumption that at least two people will occupy them. You are compensating a hotel or cruise line for losses incurred because only one person is staying in a room or cruise ship cabin.

When I first began traveling alone, I didn't know anything about this supplement, but soon began seeing it listed in different places as an additional fee. In fact, nearly all hotel and cruise pricing is based on double occupancy. When I book a hotel room, I know that I'm paying 100% of the single supplement costs, because it is a double room meant to be paid by two people, and the hotel has not lowered the price for me just because I am alone. Full price for that room means I am absorbing those costs. Many tour operators base their prices on double occupancy, too.

You can find cruises and some tour companies who advertise in favor of the solo traveler by stating upfront that there are no charges for those traveling solo. One way to find single-friendly vacations is to search by type of trip (tour, cruise or independent vacation) and destination first, and then look for travel providers that offer supplement-free journeys to the places you want to visit. Alternatively, you can look for travel providers that offer supplement-free trips first, and then choose the most appealing and affordable destination and mode of travel from that list of providers. I think the key is to start researching early after deciding on your solo destination, so you have more than enough time to plan for these additional costs, save if needed or just factor these in to your budget wisely.

While single supplement costs seem a bit unfair to those of us who are throwing fear and caution to the wind and stepping out there alone, do not let them deter you from doing it. I've been so many places alone but knowing that the financial responsibility only fell on my shoulders never kept me from going. I still book the king size bed in the large room or go on that tour if it is what I want to do. After all, experiences are currency, something that money could never equate to. Even with the things that come with traveling alone we all can afford to travel solo with a little smart budgeting before we leave. It just takes planning and getting knowledgeable about what is out there to help soften costs one we reach our destinations.

The Best Time to Go. . .

I'm asked all the time 'when is the best time to travel solo?' Great question! For some of us in the field of education, we have set vacation times that allow us to travel every year. The thing about those breaks is they tend to happen at high peak season: Spring Break, summer and winter holidays. Living in Abu Dhabi and having so many religious holiday breaks that result in long weekends or full weeks off of work has taught me about planning my trips during specific times of the year based upon my chosen location.

When I traveled to Bali, I went in October, and my driver kept telling me how blessed I was to come at that time of the year. The weather was perfect--not too hot and not rainy. The crowds were pretty non-existent compared to the spring and winter months. And most importantly, hotel and tour pricing was cheaper.

These times between peak season and low season are called "shoulder season." When you decide where you want to go, research when it is the best time to visit that location. You'll usually find information on the weather and what to expect during various tourist seasons (high, low, or shoulder). That's when that "Top Five Places I Want to Visit" list comes in handy. Traveling in the high season is better than not traveling at all but not as good as traveling when the crowds are gone. I cannot tell you how many times I've changed my mind about a location due to the sheer number of crowds that will be there or if it is monsoon season. Many people travel during the low season to avoid the crowds but may battle some weather conditions like the weather being too hot, cold, or rainy. It really can be a gamble. In some tropical areas it could technically be rainy season yet it barely rains or only rains for 30 minutes a day. Or, it could easily rain all day. As a solo traveler you have to decide if you want to take that risk. Because the itinerary you build is important to your enjoyment of the location, there's nothing worse than being holed up in your room when you have a great day of activities planned.

Traveling during the shoulder season makes most things easier for the solo traveler. The downsides, however, include certain attractions being closed until the high season when the crowds arrive. The nice part is you won't have to get up early to battle the crowds but there will still be enough tourists there to engage with others and you can relax a bit as you travel.

When researching your solo destination for the shoulder season, check the rates for hotels and the hours of operation for specific must-see sights. When the opening hours shorten, you're in the shoulder season, when hotel rates go down, you're in the low and when they rise, you're in the high season. Sometimes you can't control when your vacation falls on the calendar. But again, don't let that deter you from planning an amazing solo adventure. Pick the best place to roam after doing your research and go!

Life is too short to wait for the right time...

Transportation

7he majority of the time, flight transportation costs are the bulk of the amount that we pay for trips, especially if we are traveling abroad from America. The big three financial burdens when traveling solo are transportation, lodging and food. It is important to look for as many deals as possible to lower these initial costs so the rest of the trip itinerary can be amazing. Avid travelers tend to rely on book-it-yourself travel sites; gone are the days of having to use a travel agent to get good deals on trips, we can actually do it ourselves.

There are some sites I use often when I am beginning to plan a solo trip and want to grab good deals on flights and other aspects of my travel experience. At the start of my planning I compare prices for flights directly between airline carrier sites and travel search engines like Travelocity, Google Flights, Airfare Watchdog, Sky-Scanner, Flight Deal, and Momondo (to name a few). Most travel sites show the comparisons between prices for flights on their site versus others, so I get a good gauge for how much it costs to get to my selected location in general. Just like we do comparison shopping in our every day lives, I'm looking for the small nuances that can impact my pocketbook and the overall trip I'm trying to create. Don't be afraid to go directly to the airlines' websites to check for flights that fall into your time and financial preferences.

When traveling internationally I frequent Emirates and Etihad airlines, mainly because they are based where I live and I enjoy their service. Like most carriers, they have rewards programs that award miles for flights booked with them. If you live anywhere abroad, there are amazing carriers that are often voted the best in the world for service, comfort, reliability, and on time performance. Examples of these include Qatar Airlines, Turkish Airlines, Lufthansa, and KLM. They are also affordable. Go directly to their sites to compare prices and use the travel sites mentioned before to help you find the best service and deal combination. Many American based airlines like Delta and United have similar programs. They also reward you for use of credit cards for everyday purchases with travel miles that can be used towards trips. Many Americans take advantage of these perks when traveling from the United States to places abroad. Any way to lessen costs is key. If you can, pack light to avoid baggage fees as an additional cost. My flight to Kenya was paid by using mileage points on Etihad and made the financial costs of the rest of my trip lighter.

Another great thing about websites like Expedia are that they offer "Bundle Deals" where airfare and hotel are bundled together for cheaper rates. I use these often and have saved thousands of dollars. The only catch I've noticed is there may be limited flight times, or the options may include longer layovers in other cities before you reach your destination. Smart travelers still consider these layovers a good thing, as they can be an opportunity to get two trips out of one by getting out of the airport for the long layover and seeing the city if the visa allows. For example, my first solo trip to Barcelona included a very long layover in Istanbul. I was able to experience a great city and get good pricing on flights because I was willing to be flexible with my travel days. If that flexibility isn't feasible for you, there are plenty of flight options that honor your time on these travel sites as well.

The important thing is to set aside money and time to travel. I urge you, if you can, to remain flexible and open with travel dates if the flight times aren't ones that you initially would prefer. I typically find timings that I can work with, but if not, I use different mobile apps or websites for flights and hotels like Booking.com, Hopper, or Secret Flying to compare. When searching on these travel booking sites you can set price alerts, so you can be alerted when flight prices drop.

Seasoned travelers say there are certain days in the week when buying tickets for flights are better. Monday nights tend to be when many airlines will launch their discount promotions. This price change can help you save anywhere between 15%-25% off your ticket. If you want to take advantage of the price drops that take place on Monday night, the best time to check prices is Tuesday morning. Be sure to book your flights within a reasonable time frame between when you decide where you are going and the dates you are planning on taking the vacation, try not to wait too long. For international flights, the sooner you book the better. For domestic flights the best time to purchase is within the 21 to 42-day range (abut 3-6 weeks out) according to Skyscanner.com. Thinking of the ways to save money on initial transportation is critical, so once you make your decision on location, get right to looking around for good deals online.

Ground Transportation

Another aspect to transportation costs is transportation once on the ground. This can impact everything from hotel location and selection to itinerary planning. How will you get to the places you've listed on your Top 10 list? What if they are far from your hotel? On the ground transportation logistics is something to address in initial planning. I typically pre-arrange airport pick up when traveling alone. Since safety is paramount, it is nice to know you are set for getting around before you leave home. Use a travel itinerary planning phone app, like the Viator App, to coordinate a driver to provide round trip transport between the airport and hotel. Hiring a driver beforehand makes things so much easier and gives you a moment when you just get off the plane to get your bearings in a new place by yourself. The more planning you can handle before you travel, the better.

When I went to Tanzania, Jordan, and Indonesia I was referred to wonderful drivers/tour guides who helped me build my itineraries before I even landed in these countries. All pricing and tour planning was taken care of before I arrived which made it a smooth experience since we didn't have to haggle over rates based on what I wanted to do each day I was there. It is great to communicate your 'Must Do' lists with the drivers you use, and don't be afraid to negotiate. Let them know that you are watching your budget, and work to come up with a price that will meet both of your needs. Often times driving tourists around is their only job, and I keep this in mind as I am negotiating.

Be sure to see if the driver is knowledgeable as a guide so you can not only go to the amazing sights on your list but you can learn about them at the same time. I always request that entry costs to some of the places I want to visit be included in the amount I pay the driver if they have tour guide designation, which most of my drivers have had. For example, when I went to Petra, Jordan, which was not a cheap solo trip, I was referred to a wonderful driver and tour guide who helped me build my itinerary before I landed in Jordan. All pricing and tour planning were taken care of before I arrived which made it a smooth experience. He provided round trip airport transfer and took me to specific sites like The Lost City of Petra, Little Petra, the River Jordan, the Dead Sea, Mount Nebo, and markets. He paid entry fees into most of these places ahead of time and had tickets in hand, so I wasn't pulling out money often throughout the course of the days there for these things. At the end of my solo trips, I always try to add a tip for getting me safely around the country and sharing their insights on their homeland with me.

Drivers are great to hire for the length of trips in destinations that have a lot of driving distance between the sites on your itinerary like Bali, Jordan, Phuket, and Zanzibar. If you are like me, you want to spend your vacation enjoying the vacation, experiencing everything it has to offer, rather than spending time sitting on a long bus ride because you didn't arrange a driver to get you around faster. One thing to note is the ever-present safety piece; as a woman traveling alone it is a good idea to share your driver's name and contact information with family and friends, so they are fully aware of who you are with throughout the course of your trip. I can say that traveling with a local driver always makes me feel safer because they are usually recommended by friends or travel buddies, can easily communicate with others, know the terrain, and tend to build good relationships during the amount of time you spend with them in transit.

In most countries, drivers and tour guides are required to be registered as such. A decal is posted in their front window for you and for local authorities to easily see when you are traveling or at government checkpoints. When planning, consider use of public transportation, especially if you select a city destination that has organized transportation infrastructure in place. Public buses, subway systems, and elevated trains are very cost-effective means of on-the-ground transportation and allow you to direct funds to other aspects of the trip. Not to mention that these forms of transportation allow you to interact with the local everyday life of the city. Bangkok, London, and most cities in Europe and Asia have great public transportation systems, which can get you to and from the airport at the start and finish of your solo mission, so hiring a driver may not be necessary if you feel comfortable using these.

If you are used to using the public transit system at home this may be the route you opt to take during your solo trip. I suggest researching the transit system before you go. Find out how much it costs and how it works well in advance. This will give you more peace of mind when you begin traversing the new city on your own. Before going to a new city check to see if the transit system has an app. Find the nearest access point to the system from the hotel you are booking. In London and Paris, you must get a special transit card to access the trains. Be aware of how to get one. If you decide a bus is more your speed, I suggest getting maps for routes and sitting near the driver so you can ask questions if you think you may have made a mistake, need to get off or need information on which bus to take to get to a particular attraction in the city.

Whatever means of transport you decide, always tie it back to how it impacts the ease of your trip, because once there you will want to focus on what you are getting from the solo mission, not the logistical planning it took at the beginning when pulling it together.

Of course, there are other options to public transportation and hiring a driver. Uber has been a great way to get around as well, I've used it during my trips to Rio, Brazil and Paris. It is safer than using regular taxi services because all driver and customer location information is in the system and can be referenced at any time.

As a Black Woman I am always cognizant of my movements. I don't feel any less comfortable than I would in a regular taxi, but they seemed to be cheaper than the prices charged in taxis in those same locations. There are times where taxi drivers will quote outrageous prices if they aren't metered, so just be aware. The key is to consider all your options and always keep your comfort level regarding safety at the forefront of your decision-making process. As a woman traveling by herself, I love to walk the cities I go to on my own at first to get a feel for the city's vibe, listen to my intuition regarding my safety, and decide how I'll operate regarding how to get around (if I haven't already organized a driver). If you enjoy walking the cities you travel to, I strongly recommend doing so, but it really depends on where you've chosen to go.

When I traveled to Bali, I realized just how much distance there was between the attractions I wanted to go to there, so the driver I pre-arranged was the best option to get me to all of them. On the other hand, when I traveled to Budapest, Hungary, I soon realized that I could walk the city, be safe doing so, and hit the major attractions with no need of a driver, taxi or public transportation system. This is my preferred way to travel once I've made it to my destinations, because when you are on foot, you not only get your exercise, but you can stumble across amazing architecture, authentic local restaurants, and meet people you may not have come across if you were on a subway, train, or a bus.

I also like to take a hop-on, hop-off bus tour shortly after arriving in a new place. I find it gives me a visual overview of the layout of a city that my brain won't quite grasp from a map. These bus tours give you the freedom to explore your destination easily, by getting off at one stop seeing sights in that area and jumping back on at another stop. So much of a city can be covered this way and the costs are reasonable. When I went to Bangkok, Thailand I jumped on the hop-on, hop-off boat tour along the river, and it stopped at all the major temples along the waterway. I highly recommend looking into Hop-On, Hop Off Bus tours for the location you select when considering transportation. They are in most major cities across the globe. I was able to see many of the must-see items on my list via this mode of transportation.   I encourage you to get amongst the people as much as possible and if you are able, walk the city to get a feel for its neighborhoods, food, and vibe.

Accommodations

7me to select a hotel that meets your needs and what you are looking for in a lodging location. I tend to utilize referrals from fellow travelers who belong to the same Black travel groups I am in online for hotels, must-do attractions, night life, places to go enjoy a good meal, and tour guides/drivers they have used on their travels.

Having your hotel close in relation to the sights of the city you are going to visit is a big deal as a solo traveler. Being close lessens some of the transportation costs you may incur with transportation. It also makes being on your own and navigating a city easier. Pricing will range depending on where you go, the cost of living in that location and where you are traveling to within the city. I like that with Uber the cost of the trip will be charged to my credit card automatically, so I'm not having to take out my cash again and again when traveling on the ground. There are times where taxi drivers will quote outrageous prices, so just be aware that the key is to consider all your options and always keep your comfort level regarding safety at the forefront of your decision-making process.

I've visited Paris every year for the last three years. As a Black Woman traveling on my own, I feel comfortable being in Paris alone, and the reception the city gives me makes me feel like I could easily live there. When selecting a hotel, I think of the areas of the city I want to frequent, like the Louvre, Eiffel Tower, or shopping along the Champs Elysees. Since I am alone, I often want to be close to major attractions depending on my trip's purpose, although hotels near major attractions can be a little more expensive because they are close to the action. Paris has a sound public transportation system so I try to make not e of the metro stations. If the hotel is near a major transit hub, that is an added perk!

Some solo travelers select hostels, which provide them not only with a cheaper place to stay, but an opportunity to meet other travelers, as it is more communal than a traditional hotel. Hostels carry the stigma of being cheaper options, with little to none of the amenities we are used to finding in traditional hotels. They often aren't viewed as clean or safe, but many cases they actually are. Many share mixed reviews about using hostels. If you decide that the hostel route is the one you would like to go, I can't stress enough the need to research the hostel and its location in the city thoroughly. Read the reviews of other travelers. Researching to ensure the area is safe is major because you are a woman traveling on your own. This is a fact that must be at the forefront of your mind.

You will hear me tell you to do your research a lot in this guide. It's always better to make informed decisions, especially regarding accommodations as that is a major part of your stay. When selecting flights, try to book one that lands in the afternoon, so you can get to your lodging during the daylight hours and can make any necessary changes during the daytime rather than having to switch at night. Again, read the reviews from other travelers about their experiences with the choice of hotel. Consider their feedback on the location in relation to important things in the city, amenities, overall quality of service, cleanliness, dining, and vibe.

Boutique Hotels

One type of accommodation I've come to love are boutique hotels. I love a good boutique hotel experience. I've found that I enjoy them even more than large resorts or hotel chains. These hotels provide a more unique vibe to travelers and aren't so big that the personal touch is lost trying to meet the needs of hundreds of customers. They are much smaller and are considered "trendy." Much of the time there is a theme that is carried throughout boutique hotels that make them charming and "different" than the usual hotel. When looking for lodging don't be afraid to try one! When I solo travel, I like to feel like everything I need is at my fingertips should I choose to partake; for example, fitness center, great pool, room service, and the opportunity to book tours through the hotel if desired. With a hostel and Airbnb, you lose those options most of the time.

Airbnb

Staying in an Airbnb as a solo traveler isn't a bad option, most often than not it's someone's personal property so there is a certain "feel" of home there, they are usually clean, and you aren't sharing with others. Pricing for Airbnb is usually very good, and you can find great properties in amazing locations all around the world. Follow the same steps you would when selecting any type of accommodation: research the area, see the location of the Airbnb in relation to the major attractions you are interested in, search the Airbnb site for information on the host and read the reviews about the property.

Another perk of renting an Airbnb is that you will be able to save on food costs because you can go to the grocery store and cook for yourself whenever the budget calls for it. It just depends on the type of traveler you are; one who likes to have your needs provided the entire length of your vacation, or one who doesn't mind doing for yourself at times. A lot of rented homes in Southeast Asia provide a chef who will prepare not only breakfast but can be hired for the length of your stay if so desired, and all for reasonable costs! This is a very common thing there, especially in Bali and Thailand. Just another reason Southeast Asia is a great place to begin your solo travels.

In recent years there have been creation of short-term rental platforms like Airbnb, such as Noirebnb, which was created to ensure that no discriminatory practices were taking place when renting, all travelers feel welcome and receive a safe and inclusive travel experience. The platform runs very similar to Airbnb, but the travel experience of people of color is considered, as their website describes itself as "a concierge service, accommodations provider and experience curator specifically created to procure safe and stress-free travel for the African Diaspora." As a Black female solo traveler, that description sits well with me. Noirebnb is an option to be considered because it is a source that would be familiar to what I experience my needs are as a person of color.

Every traveler is different, and depending on the type of traveler you are, whichever route you take, be sure to ask questions and research so that you can make informed decisions. All in all, choosing the right fit in lodging is an important part of your trip, as it will be your home base for the length of your stay, and you will need to feel comfortable and safe while there.

All - Inclusive Resort

There are many options for lodging that we don't tend to think of often when planning for a solo vacation. One of those is heading to an all-inclusive resort because these typically are frequented by larger groups, couples, and families--not the woman on a solo vacay. In fact, all-inclusive resorts are a great option for the solo traveler because everything is taken care of; all your food, drinks, even some activities are a part of the package you pay for upfront, so it literally takes a lot of the planning out of your hands. This helps you focus on just enjoying the vacation as it comes. All-inclusive resorts can be the solo traveler's perfect getaway.

I recall a solo staycation I did at an all-inclusive resort in Ras Al Khaimah, United Arab Emirates. I needed a moment away from the rigors of work that was getting intense and decided to go for a bit of rejuvenation. It was nice to know everything was handled. My time was still my own, and I could leave the resort if I wanted to do an excursion. The option to live the full resort experience from the unlimited drinks to the night club on site was my own. Not to mention the all you can eat buffets were amazing. I suggest looking into all-inclusive options when planning your solo vacay, especially if you are a woman on a mission to give herself a break from all of the responsibilities that come with running households, businesses, and the sheer busy-ness that comes with our lives. Let someone else handle it!

The question is what's the best way to go solo at an all-inclusive resort where there are likely to be a lot of families and large groups? How can you make the best use of your time and get the most out of the experience? The key to going to an all-inclusive resort as a solo traveler is to know what you want out of your vacation and how to get it. Remember, knowing 'why' you're going can help you with knowing what you want when you get there! Here are some tips I've picked up when I've done solo missions at these kinds of accommodations.

- *Get Informed* - When I check-in I typically ask reception what they recommend for on-site activities, where the quietest spots on the resorts are, what the fitness center and spa hours are and if there are any specials on spa services. I also ask about the restaurants and if there are any on site night clubs or bars. It's important to ask about the type of experience you want to create for yourself when you first arrive.

- *Be Social* – Sometimes all-inclusive resorts will have happy hours. Depending on if you've planned to be social this vacation, you can start by going to the happy hour for a cocktail. This gives you an opportunity to meet other travelers, maybe even ones traveling solo like you.

- *Me Time* – I really enjoy my private time. Being alone is so settling for me. It helps me clear my head, relax, unwind and quiet the chaos that the busy-ness of my life. I encourage you to take some alone time. Go sit on the beach and catch the sunset, grab your book and read in a cabana or on your balcony. Take some moments to just do you.

- *Massage on Deck* – I love massages. When I go to Southeast Asia, I get a massage every day, granted they are extremely cheap and really good! Many of us are not able to get massages in our regular everyday lives, so I encourage you to make it a practice to do so when you solo travel. For many of us part of the purpose of traveling solo is to experience things we don't normally and find ways to connect with the world outside our own. When you go to Bali, try a traditional Balinese massage, when in Thailand, get a $9 full body massage, and when staying in an all-inclusive resort, enjoy a splurge with an expensive spa treatment. Allow yourself to be spoiled. Pamper yourself!

• *Enjoy Day and Nighttime Entertainment* - On most all-inclusive resorts there is entertainment to be enjoyed as many do not leave the resort at all for the length of their stay. While I encourage taking a day trip somewhere off the property, enjoying what is provided there is also a plus. Participate in activities like water sports, volleyball or tennis, cooking lessons or learning about local crafts. Activities like these are almost always included on resorts. Many resorts will also organize day tours off site. These are awesome because you get a moment in a new environment and meet other travelers who are staying at the resort that you may connect with and meet up with for dinner or a drink later in the day. There are many opportunities to mix and mingle day and night, even if it's at the swim up bar at the resort. When I went to the Dominican Republic there were so many activities happening around the pool every day, you could choose to get involved with the foam party at the main pool or stay to yourself at one of the quieter pools away from the masses. Either way, get out of your room and get involved in something while there! At nighttime, plan at least one night to take in the evening entertainment. The beauty of all of this is that you can do everything provided or nothing at all, and can change your mind in an instant, depending on the vacation you've envisioned for yourself.

Excursions

*S*ee new things   *&*
*C*reate new memories.

*D*estinations are all about the people, foods and things to see and do there. Many people like to try new things from foods to bucket list activities that they may not have considered ever doing before. This is where creative itinerary planning comes in! Depending on the vibe of the location that you've selected, there are no shortage of adventurous and relaxed activities that you can choose from. Have patience. Even as an experienced solo traveler, every time I start a new trip it takes me a day or two to get solo stable – to shed those initial nerves of being out there on my own managing all the details, logistics and documents. Be patient with yourself as you work to get over those initial jitters that are there reminding you that you're by yourself. Give it a moment, you'll find your strength. I do want to encourage you not to sleep in, but to push yourself to get up and out there to create new memories. There will be days when you really don't want to get up early because you're tired, but those are the ones I encourage you to do so, because you don't remember how tired you were during a trip, you remember what you did. You will be happy that you forced yourself to get up and get engaged with the location you picked for your solo mission.

I remember being physically exhausted in Milan. I scheduled a walking tour of the city for the following day and already had it in my mind to skip it so I could sleep in the next day. When my alarm went off for the tour, I was still tired but weighed my options and it hit me, you came here to see new things and create new memories that can't be done in a hotel room. I'm glad I got up because I got to scratch off a "Lived List" activity of mine: I saw Davinci's Last Supper. Such an unreal moment.

Trust me, there will be time in your vacation to be lazy, but the things you'll remember are the activities you organize for yourself. Get up early and see that sunrise, tour that cathedral, see the temples, hike to the waterfall, and have that authentic local meal. These are the things the best solo missions consist of: *moments.* You're going to be thankful that you got up early and saw that church, went on that hike to the waterfall, met those people, and had that meal. In the moment, it seems like it's going to be difficult, but the memories made from a full day are totally worth it.

A lot of your excursion activity choices have to do with the type of traveler you are, as well as, what the location you've selected is famous for. Those things will guide your itinerary planning. Earlier in this guide I suggested researching activities and creating a "Top 10 Must Dos" list for your vacation. That list may be things you've heard you must see when traveling there, and it could include restaurants that should not be missed. Traveling opens the mind to the possibilities of trying new things, from foods to more adventurous activities. The beauty of it is you never know what you'd try until you get there.

A prime example from my life is that I've always been the girl who didn't enjoy anything associated with heights, i.e. roller coasters, ferris wheels, or even standing on the top of mountains. Just wasn't me. Once I began going on solo missions and realizing that there was nothing to fear out here in the world, I began doing more and more adventurous activities whilst on vacation. Pretty soon you could find me in Rio jumping off mountains with a kite on my back or climbing hills to feel the rush of excitement and accomplishment at the top of cliffs. I share that story because that one adventurous act opened me up to trying new things on vacation--things I'd once feared for no good reason.

When I traveled to Thailand, I zip lined across the forest, in Bali, I got on the Bali swing well above the ground, and in Ghana I conquered canopy walks above the rain forest. Don't get me wrong, I also like to do more relaxing activities on vacation like dinner cruises along major waterways, visiting important cultural sites like temples, and eating local foods I won't easily find at home. For me, planning a variety of fun and exciting excursions that provide me with a sense of the location I'm visiting is paramount. The key is to mix them up, consider safety precautions, and have fun.

Some of the best excursions I've taken while traveling solo have been cultural experiences. Every location has something unique and special about it; the culture. Even the United States, with its abundance of diversity has an underlying culture that can be felt when you travel domestically. I strongly encourage you to plan for immersing yourself into the local customs and culture of your location. Local dance and cooking classes, cocktail making classes, drumming lessons, street art walks, creating your own food tour to restaurants known for their local delicacies, attending traditional ceremonies or shows, even rolling cigars are some of the cool things you can get in to that are direct connections to the culture of the destinations I've visited.

If you are traveling to destinations where travel insurance is highly recommended, I do suggest getting it. I don't always purchase travel insurance, but it is just a good idea to do whether traveling solo or with groups, especially if you know that you plan on trying new things or are in countries where loss of property due to theft or crime rates against persons nationally may be high. Depending upon what policy you choose to fit your needs they aren't very expensive, but can cover you should you need hospital stay, other types of bodily injury or illness, specific pieces of personal property like cameras or lap tops, and give you peace of mind when you go abroad. Insurance also covers you for illnesses that may happen where you are traveling to.

For example, I purchased travel insurance when I went to Rio de Janeiro because the safety advisories warned that the rate of theft there is very high. When you decide on a destination your initial research into the location is very important, especially for a Black woman who is traveling by herself. I cannot stress enough the need to take safety precautions before you travel. If some of your items are stolen either by a pickpocket or at your hotel, make sure that you have copies of:

- Your travel itinerary
- Passport
- Visa
- Vaccination documents
- Credit/Debit Cards
- Bank information

with a friend at home and in an electronic cloud. When going it alone you should invest in travel insurance against theft should it be your phone or other item that goes missing. I also suggest taking a photo of your expensive gear before you leave in case you need to make a claim. When you are a solo traveler planning on doing extreme activities like zip lining, sky diving, hang/para gliding, or bungee jumping, you must cover yourself. Travel insurance companies will have you sign no liability waivers, so protecting yourself is extremely important. Depending upon the policy you choose your physical body and possessions are covered for any unforeseen occurrences that may happen abroad. While we don't always like to focus on what could happen, being ready for anything makes the vacation better.

When I traveled to Rio, Brazil and Accra, Ghana I purchased travel insurance because I knew that I would be doing some adventurous activities in these locations. Zip lining and hang gliding were at the top of my list and walking along a small wooden bridge above the canopy of the rainforest. If you are the type to select these kinds of activities when you travel, get that insurance. I use World Nomads Insurance, but there are many others that you can find online, including on Traveling Black Women website. The company will email the policy you select immediately upon purchase. For some of us, extreme sports are not our thing, and we tend to opt for more grounded excursions when traveling.

After taking in all that the city has to offer, I like to review what is left on my itinerary and add items or take them away depending on where my head is at and how I'm feeling. If you've done a few adventurous excursions and feel the need for rest and relaxation, listen to that feeling and do it.

Personal Safety

raveling safely is the one major thing that stops people from traveling solo. The stories we hear on the
news or the ideas we have about certain parts of the
world work against the natural inclination we have to explore
outside of our comfort zones.

For a long time, I was hesitant to travel by myself. Before I
left the United States to live abroad, you would never find me
without at least one other traveler at my side. Call it fear of the
unknown, discomfort with leaving what I am familiar with, or
just being street smart, you would not catch me venturing too
far from home by myself.

There is nothing wrong with this way of thinking, we know
that things happen while traveling all the time. But the thing to
remember is that things can happen whether you are traveling
solo or in a group, so letting fear take control is something I
want to encourage you to let go. The key is to plan well and
communicate those plans to others. When I travel on my own,
my family back home knows what I plan to do, and I keep them
abreast of my itinerary before leaving. Send copies of your
proposed itinerary as soon as flights, hotels and excursions

are booked prior to leaving on your trip. If changes are made during the trip, send family and trusted friends the activity information, so they are aware of what your plans look like for the days abroad. This works to give everyone a piece of mind.

Make copies of your travel documents, especially your passport. I tend to carry around the copy of my passport in a plastic sandwich bag (to keep it from getting wet) and leave my passport locked in the hotel safe. Whatever you feel most comfortable doing is fine, just be sure to carry some form of official documentation with you when out and about. Leave a copy of your passport with someone back at home as well. I also note where the U.S. Embassy is in relation to my hotel and carry a small card with the contact information on it for the Embassy. It's just good practice to be aware of who is there to help you should it be needed.

If you're a US citizen, you can also sign up with the Smart Traveler Enrollment Program (STEP), which assists travelers in case of emergency. Just because you aren't in the States doesn't mean you don't have support when away. The more people who are aware of your location, the better.

I get the question often from travelers: "Should I take my passport with me at all times or should I leave it at the hotel?" It really is a personal decision, and knowing the importance of that document, many want to keep it close. I tend to leave my valuables at my hotel. Once I've made it through customs, I don't need my passport anymore, but I will need it to get back home. As a solo traveler you must think of safety a little more than those who are in groups, and unfortunately that means being extra cautious about what you take with you into the city you are visiting.

When packing I carry a purse that is worn across my shoulder, to keep it from being easily taken off me. This happens in many places--people riding past you on scooters, grabbing your bag if it isn't secure, and riding off. Sometimes people leave their bags in taxis or other forms of transportation as well. I practice the rule of "looking back," where I always turn around and check the area I was sitting in when leaving a taxi, my seat at a restaurant, or any space where I've been for any length of time. I check for my most important items every time I stand up to move on. These are my wallet, phone, and passport/passport copy.

My suggestion? Lock your passport in the safe or a locked suitcase in the hotel room and keep a copy of it on your phone or on you. If you don't have a luggage lock or room safe, you can ask the front desk at the hotel to keep things of value in their main hotel safety deposit box. The other good part of putting items in the hotel deposit box is they are usually liable for anything that disappears from the front desk safe. Passports and very expensive items really don't need to be carried on you unless you are using them for a purpose. Nonetheless, whatever you decide is a personal decision, just remember to take precautions either way.

Pickpockets

When you're traveling out of the hotel for the day, keep your expensive gadgets well-concealed and in pockets or bags that are not easily accessible to pickpockets. Unfortunately, pickpocketing is a big thing in some places, so be very careful about where your items are and never carry more money than you need.

I've invested in a slim money belt that fits under my clothes which comes in handy when I don't want to carry a backpack or fanny pack. Many stores also have more stylish looking money belts that contain hidden compartments. Just be mindful about looking like you're carrying a lot of cash, you don't need to call any unwanted attention to yourself. Be aware when in very crowded places like markets, train stations, and large public events of your surroundings. Monitor who is in your personal space as these are the types of places that pickpockets love. Your purse should have a flap and a zipper. If you insist on carrying a wallet in your pocket, it should be a front pocket not in the back.

I've found that wearing pickpocket proof clothing has eased my concern over this happening to me. Don't just pack for cute outfits, pack for function. I specifically pack pants with zippered pockets inside of pockets, bras with stash pockets for money, and jackets with inside pockets. These are all great places to keep cash.

Be careful around warning signs about pickpockets. If you see a sign in a public place warning you about pickpockets don't call attention to where your money or valuables are by checking them, as pickpockets are always watching and will get an idea of where you are keeping these things. Be vigilant and try to call the least amount of attention to yourself as possible when on a solo mission.

When I traveled to Paris I met up with a friend for the day. She had her suitcase and a purse that was unzipped, and she did not realize it was open. As we were leaving the Metro station a person casually bumped into her, apologized and kept moving. About 10 minutes later when we reached the café for lunch, she realized her wallet was gone. She was the victim of a pickpocket and didn't even realize it happened in the moment.

The stress of canceling cards, being abroad with no money, and losing her identification took all her enthusiasm about the trip away. She ended up leaving early to head back home. Be aware, make sure your bags are closed, and that you've taken steps to secure your valuables.

Blending In

Blending in with the locals is a good way to become a part of the place you've traveled to and makes you less of a target for would be thieves or people who want to take advantage of a tourist. One of the best solo women travel tips I've heard was that the first thing you should do when reaching your destination is to go into a local store (like a drugstore or market) and just buy something small so you can have the bag, and that bag marks you as a local. Simply genius! I always look at what the locals wear in any given city that I travel to, because the less I look like a tourist the less likely I will call attention to myself. I also look at maps before leaving my hotel room so I can get a sense of where I am going or what areas I'm in. Of course, there will be times where you will pull the map out whilst walking the city but having some prior knowledge of the area will help call less attention to yourself.

When I arrive to my destination, I buy a local SIM card for my unlocked smartphone at the airport so that I ca have 4G data coverage and can use Google Maps when exploring the city. This keeps me from taking out maps and looking like a tourist, especially since I am alone. My experience with purchasing SIM cards in the many places I've been, is that they are actually affordable and a great way to stay connected. I highly recommend getting one.

Trust Your Intuition

As a woman, always being mindful of your surroundings is critical. Trust that women's intuition we've been blessed with when situations arise. If you meet other travelers or locals and something isn't "sitting right" in your gut, listen to it and dismiss yourself from the situation. Remember, everyone doesn't need to know you are solo.

A couple years ago I traveled across Italy by train. My first stop was in Venice, Italy. It is such a stunning location. The architecture and food are wonderful, and the people are very friendly. On that trip I noticed that the locals I interacted with at shops, restaurants and cafes were warm and welcoming. They enjoyed the fact that I was a Black American woman. I was asked to dinner, to hang out at local watering holes, and to experience the nightlife there. While I feel like I can hold my own in most situations and don't find myself operating in fear when traveling alone, there were times when my intuition kicked in and I felt uncomfortable. I've learned to act on that feeling, and so I found myself either suggesting lunchtime meals or declined the invitations altogether. Never be rushed into a decision when it means your safety is put into question. Take your time and consider all the cons of the decision you are being asked to make. Meeting with new friends in public places during the day is much safer than venturing out with them to unknown spots at night. I tend to let people know where I am going if I've decided that I am going to go out at nighttime.

If you're out partying, be sure to watch your intake so your judgment isn't impaired. I also always suggest ordering all your drinks yourself and keeping them with you. It's important to remember that while meeting new people is one of the best parts of solo travel, when you make decisions no one is there to know the particulars, so if you do accept be sure to share your plans with family and friends back home so your whereabouts are known at all times. As my grandmother always used to say, "better safe than sorry."

It is important that women remember that we can control a lot of what happens during our trips alone by staying alert and aware. The steps I mentioned previously are just a few that you can take to feel more comfortable when you're in an unfamiliar place. One best practice for women that will ensure you have a better, happier time is not telling strangers you're alone. When you meet other travelers or locals, never make it known that you are a solo traveler, instead use phrases in conversation that give the impression you are traveling with others. Saying things like, "my friends are loving the excursions we did today," or "my friends are meeting me later" when chatting with people. Even though this isn't true, it still gives the impression that you aren't alone, and that other people are going to be expecting you. Don't tell people you meet where you're staying, it should be your safe zone and always carry the business card for your hotel on you.

Many Black women who take care of themselves every day in the world are cautious of who we entertain and the choices we make when going out, whether it be during the daytime or at night. As a forty-something, I've been through my fair share of difficult situations, be it at home or abroad, and I can't stress enough the need to be vigilant at all times, especially if you are young.

One rule of thumb I hold myself to, be it day or nighttime, is keeping it public. I stick to public spaces where many people are around, which gives you a level of comfort that no one will be able to easily take advantage of the fact that you are alone.

It's true that all women should be careful, especially alone, but there are a couple of reasons that I make this point.

Most older women have many life experiences under our belts, so we may think differently about the places we find ourselves in or the things we chose to do. Older women may opt not to go out at night to experience the nightlife as much as younger women, simply because we've experienced it a lot over the years and it isn't as appealing to us anymore.

When traveling solo, going out to experience your location at nighttime is perfectly fine, but we must keep in mind that just like at home in the States, many things can happen under the cover of darkness. I've traveled a lot in my twenties and in my forties and I can confirm that I received a lot more attention, appreciated and otherwise, in my twenties.

If you are a young woman you may need to be more careful about unsavory characters than us more mature women. At the end of the day whether you are young or seasoned, as a woman alone you must listen to that voice of discernment when venturing out to entertain at certain times of the day and night. Trust your instincts.

Nonetheless, one of the things I like best about solo travel is that it is social (if you allow it to be). The key is to stay open to meeting others while watching your own back. Most of us have private and social parts to our personalities. I'm willing to bet this is the reason you are on this solo venture in the first place, because you have no problem being on your own and can easily gauge when and where you want to engage with others. This makes for the best solo traveler!

I enjoy meeting people and a lot of the times I take the first step to do so. I think that taking control of who you meet can be a good thing as you tend to make good decisions when you are the one determining who will be in your space. For this reason, I tend to size up all my options and choose who I'll chat with on my solo ventures. I never assume that women are safe just because they are a woman.

Always exercise your gift of discernment when interacting with others, but don't travel with your guard up the entire trip. Allow yourself to meet others. It's one of my favorite parts of solo travel; you meet people in ways you never would have otherwise. Connecting with locals or other travelers early on in your travels can make a world of difference in what you do, what attractions you visit, and the overall quality of the solo experience. Trust your gut when interacting with others. Some good friends have been met through my travels, and if I never allowed myself to meet them, they wouldn't be in my life. So go ahead and be social, just be smart!

There will be times where you may need to remind others of exactly who you are while traveling. By that I mean that you aren't someone to be taken advantage of just because you are a woman and traveling alone. Don't be afraid to be direct if necessary. Don't get me wrong, I was raised to be polite with everyone I meet. However, I have a way of politely making myself understood should "difficult" situations arise. When it comes to safety, if polite doesn't work I allow myself to be more direct—especially when I travel solo. While I encourage you to be as polite as possible with others you meet along your journeys, the reality is you are a Black woman traveling alone, and you must ensure you are completely understood an your boundaries are respected.

Realistically you won't have to do this often, as most will be completely respectful of your space and wishes, but it has happened a couple of times over the course of my solo travels.

Nightlife as a Solo Traveler

*T*hroughout this guide I've been stressing the need to be aware of your surroundings because as a woman traveling alone, you can be the object of unwanted attention at times. Yes, safety is a priority, especially when going out at night, but it doesn't mean that as a solo traveler you have to stay at the hotel or even close to it when you want to get out and be social. There are plenty of activities that women traveling alone can get into at night while still exercising those safety precautions I discussed earlier.

Here are a few that I have enjoyed on my many travels alone:

Performing Arts

Have you thought of going to a play, the opera or symphony? These 3 activities have been on my "Lived List" for some time now so I took advantage of being in Paris and taking in a show there. It stands as one of my favorite cities and I have always wanted to attend an opera at the famous Opera Bastille House there.

Since I have been to Paris solo for the past 3 years, I took the opportunity to attend one. It is a such a beautiful space and you really feel the levels of sophistication that come with seeing an opera there. I highly recommend going to the opera, symphony or a play abroad. It is really such a nice evening event that is filled with culture. You'll be around people but at the same time will be allowed to enjoy the performance in your own way. Truly an elegant night out, and there is no need to know the language to enjoy the performance.

Dinner w/ a Local Family

One of the best experiences I've had on a solo trip was enjoying dinner at my driver's home. Because you are spending a lot of time with them in over the course of your trip, you will most likely develop a good relationship with them. What I've found in many of the countries I've visited is that people are so warm and welcoming, and they want you to experience their lives and culture, especially through food. I hope that you are able to develop a level of trust with your driver, so if offered, you can feel comfortable enough to accept an invite to break bread with their family.

That is a huge thing, being asked to meet wives and children and partake in local foods at their home! I experienced this in Jordan when I visited the Lost City of Petra. My driver was amazing and one of the kindest people you'd ever meet. I was flattered that he felt I should meet his wife and children. It was a great evening spent with amazing people.

Be open to enjoying an evening with your driver experiencing their family or even a bite to eat at a local restaurant that they recommend.

Night Museums

I always go to museums on my travels. I'm a history junkie and seeing relics and learning from the past is my thing. Museums hold so much rich history about the place I'm at and some of my "Must Do" sights are housed there (think the Mona Lisa or Michelangelo's Statue of David). If you find that you enjoy visiting museums when you travel, I suggest using this to your advantage, especially if you want to get out and about for an evening activity. Push back the timing for your museum visit until later (depending upon the closing hours of the museum of course). Some museums close at 8:00 pm, so you can plan a nice evening there and then catch a meal afterwards. I also suggest visiting art galleries that are also open in the evenings in some cities if art is an interest of yours. Watch for the hours and build your museum or gallery time into your evening.

Festivals & Street Markets

Festivals and street markets are always present in most cities, especially during the summer or when the locals are celebrating a memorable period in the life of the country. If you know that you would like to participate in a festival to get a real feel for the city or culture where you are, I suggest going where the action is. Whether it's a night street market or a local festival, connect with the front desk at your hotel to find out what is currently happening there. Before I travel solo to any destination, I go online to check out what's going on in terms of public events and watch the locals in action. These nights are always filled with a lot of people, so they are very public. Just be mindful of your surroundings and be sure to follow my safety tips when being in very crowded places. Be aware, be smart, but have fun!

Meet-Ups

Meet up with fellow travelers from your online travel groups who may be in the same city when you are and get involved in public evening events that are going on around the city. Some of them may be solo and looking to get around like-minded people for a night as well. You can keep it simple and just go for dinner, drinks, and a bit of dancing at a club. You may even decide to attend a concert, go to a jazz lounge, or partake in an evening food tour. The options are endless! Meeting up with others who have decided to step out on their own feels great and can lead to meeting up with them another time on the same trip or in a different destination at another time in the year. When I went to Paris I met up with a fellow traveler and we joined a night tour. Many cities offer these, and it could be something simple like a walking tour to "haunted" areas of the city or a cruise along a major waterway. Meet-ups are great because you can develop bonds that last well beyond the initial meeting.

Evening Stroll

The more you travel on your own you will see how much you value your quiet time. Maybe your life back home is filled with many commitments to others and you tend to get lost in the midst of it. We know this happens with Black women, because we are running things in our regular lives. I find that I really enjoy going for a walk, especially in the evening. Walking at night is very different from walking during the day because daytime walking is usually for a specific purpose, you're on a mission to get to those must- see sights, or you're a part of a walking tour of the city. Evening walks are more laid back, and they give you a sense of calm, because you are reclaiming moments that have somehow been taken from you back home. Some cities are great for walking at night. I enjoyed walking during the evening in Budapest, Venice, Paris, and Bali, just enjoying the energy of the people around me. Of course, you have to be careful where you walk at night, but this is truly a great way to spend an evening on your solo trip.

Loneliness

vs.

Being Alone

"*The man who goes alone can start today; but he who travels with another must wait until that other is ready.*"

-Henry David Thoreau

7aveling with family and friends is the traditional way to travel. We collectively decide where we want to go and what we want to do and the days are typically packed with an awesome, yet tiring itinerary. When you're with a group, the trend is typically one to fill the time with as much as possible. I mean, you didn't travel to sit around, right? This is never a bad thing, and many opt only to travel with others because they can't imagine experiencing the feeling of being alone or lonely while on holiday.

I think it is important to recognize that there is a difference between being alone and being lonely. Being alone requires a conscious decision. You are deciding that you want to spend time with yourself, to get in touch with yourself, and to see what you need from you, with no distractions. Being lonely on the other hand, is a feeling. It's those moments when you recognize that you desire to have someone else's presence amongst yours, and if we are completely honest, it doesn't feel so good.

So, what happens as a solo traveler when you value your alone moments but feel pangs of loneliness? I am here to tell you they will happen, although less and less the more you do it. Every solo vacation I've taken has held a bout of loneliness. We are human after all. Black women are notoriously known for being strong and independent, but we have our moments too. As I've gotten more used to being alone and valuing my own company, those lonely moments have lessened. When they don't, my advice is to simply get around people. Fight the urge to stay in the hotel room, on social media or Facetime, get out and about.

I like to wander the streets, hop on public transportation, stop in cathedrals, buy street food near markets, and get a bit lost. It can be a bit scary to travel on your own, and even lonely at times, but the best way to get past the initial loneliness is to put yourself out there. Head to the hotel restaurant or a local spot you may have heard rave reviews about and surround yourself with people. Sometimes I strike up conversation, other times I just people watch, which I absolutely love to do, and the feeling passes. That's the great thing about feelings, they will soon subside, they don't last forever.

When I traveled to Zanzibar, Tanzania on my own I had some moments like these. There will be those times when you wish a specific person were there sharing the experience with you, or just having someone familiar to talk to. Completely normal. You can get around others or even call or Facetime loved ones if it gets to be a lot. I've found the feeling will fade and you'll be back to enjoying your "me" time. What I've noticed is that when we travel in groups, we tend to be so caught up in the happenings within the group that we can miss out on interacting with local people or miss moments altogether.

I was in Zanzibar and I decided to get something to eat at a local restaurant. I ended up striking up conversation with a young Black man who was traveling solo as well. It turned out he was from Canada and was in the process of traveling from the southernmost tip of Africa to the northernmost tip. I was so impressed with his story and have shared it with many since. When I think about how I could have missed the opportunity to meet a fellow traveler on such an ambitious journey because I was lost in the midst of a group or keeping to myself, I am thankful for the inclination to combat any bouts of loneliness with meeting others. You never know who you will meet in those moments.

I value my alone time, because no energy is being tapped by others for their own needs. I'm able to center myself and my focus squarely on me. This time is mine to recharge and recalibrate, so when I return from my holiday, I am ready to give my energy to others again. As Black women we give a lot of ourselves to work and family, the needs of others, and don't check in to our own needs. I deliberately choose to be alone when I need to check in with my own needs and I value that time so much.

Society tells us that we are our best when surrounded by others. This narrative typically drives women to seek companionship for most trips abroad. While this isn't all bad, it can make us miss out on the moments that our solitude can help develop growth, change and a new level of independence. I would venture to argue that solo travel continually "grows" you for life.

Don't get me wrong, I believe that many milestone moments should be shared with those you love, but there is a reason 90% of my travel is solo. For one, I value the time where I silence the world and quiet the chaos. When others are with you, you are always "on" and don't have the opportunity to self-reflect and recharge your own batteries because energy is constantly being tapped from you.

I often hear women say that they wouldn't travel to what are deemed as "romantic" locations like the Maldives because they are "saving them" for when they can go with their husband or boyfriend. If that position suits you, who am I to argue it? There are many more places to travel solo that a few can be reserved for travel with a special someone.

I used to be of this mindset, the infamous "bae-cation" to beautiful tropical islands or cozy winter retreats would wait so I wouldn't have to experience it alone. One day as I began planning for another solo excursion it hit me, if not now, when? Waiting for someone to travel with would be nice, but we miss out on experiences when we continue to wait for others to impact what we do. Life is too short to wait for anything.

So imagine this... It's day 3 of your first solo mission and you've been pretty much completely alone with your thoughts the entire trip. That time has been broken up with the occasional itinerary activity to one of the must-see sights of the location, but you've been alone primarily the whole time since touching down. Eventually pangs of loneliness start to creep in and you begin to wonder if traveling by yourself was the best choice. What do you do? The "woman empowered, do it on your own" talk sounds great, and in theory it is, but for those going off into the world for first time as a solo traveler it can feel a bit naïve. Or is it?

Here are a few things I do to fight the feelings of loneliness and boredom while on my own...

I stay open to being spontaneous and curious. The best solo trips I've taken were the ones where I took charge of my time, emotions, and fears and stepped headfirst into the culture and activities of my destination.

On Day 1 I usually give myself a moment to get adjusted to where I am and take it slow. I don't plan any itinerary outings for that day, and I talk to the hotel activity planner, concierge or front desk to get an idea of what they recommend I do over the course of my stay. Essentially, I try to find my way by asking questions and getting to know the people I'm talking to by asking for advice. Be it asking for the best coffee or restaurant in town, art galleries and museums or whatever you are passionate about. This will not only enrich your experience, but it can provide a safety net of sorts in case you run into any trouble over the course of the stay. It's building a community of people who know you in a place where you know no one, that can support you if and when you may need it, even just for a brief conversation during one of those "lonely moments" we spoke of earlier.

It's always good to get information from locals, especially those connected to your hotel. Oftentimes they can recommend something that an be arranged through the hotel for later in your vacation. Connect with the locals from the get-go. Getting to know the hotel staff helps to break the ice of a new location when you are traveling alone and opens the doors to new experiences. Don't be afraid to do so but trust your instincts and remain vigilant in your dealings with those you meet along the way.

Solo traveling challenges you to try different experiences that you normally wouldn't do, and with the advice from those you've met along the way, you can have a dope experience that is spontaneous and fun. Something fun that can lend itself to beating the loneliness is giving yourself an assignment like finding the best burger in town, a specific cocktail that you heard the city is famous for, or catching the best flamenco show in Barcelona. Kind of like a traveler's scavenger hunt. These activities lend themselves to you meeting locals and other travelers as you move through your list. This will help you to feel more connected to others while enjoying the peace that solo travel brings too.

Going off to travel on your own is already taking yourself out of your comfort zone, so be sure to trust your gut and listen to your emotions when trying new things. If something doesn't feel right, trust it. Be it trying new foods or doing an activity like bungee jumping or zip lining from very high heights, if you're feeling extremely unsure, don't do it. I encourage you to throw on your backpack and head out to explore your surroundings, challenge yourself some and create new and improved "comfort zones." Most importantly you should allow yourself to enjoy the freedom that traveling alone gives; you can do exactly what you want to do. Solo travel can be an enlightening experience, especially if you enjoy your own company.

No matter if you're nibbling on plantain in Ghana or learning how to salsa in Rio, one of the most beautiful parts of traveling is becoming mesmerized by fascinating sights and flavors. Allowing yourself to be spontaneous and curious is a part of the solo travelers' journey, while exercising your street smarts to stay safe of course. To fully immerse yourself in the moment requires a healthy level of trust. I can't encourage you enough to immerse yourself into the local culture. Allow yourself time to meet others and find out everything that your location has to offer. Build an itinerary that includes traditional cooking and dance classes, take food tours, go bike riding through the city, visit local artists and musicians and take an art or drumming class, take photo walks to iconic spots for great pictures with travel groups you meet up with throughout your trip, go to historical landmarks and plan something exciting and out of the norm for you that is central to the culture you are visiting.

Attend local carnivals or celebrations and even get involved in one. Taste the food they love, try their dance moves and find out what they are most proud of. Believe me, this will make your solo experience one to remember for years to come and keep the loneliness and boredom that may creep in away. I've found that when I let myself loose, I've met some friends for life and created memories I will never forget, and it all started with the decision to go off on my own.

Figure out the ways you enjoy spending time alone. For me, I like to plan a productive solo day. This may include writing, reading that book that I've had trouble finding the time to get in to real life, relaxing in my room or by the pool or beach, getting a massage, or just taking a moment to "do me" with no rush of an activity to get to. It's important as a solo traveler to figure out your alone time joys because they will make your trip that much more exciting and allows you to connect with yourself. Decide what that looks like for you and make sure to carve some time out for that activity. It could be reading, beach days, long bubble baths or catching up on your favorite shows.

Because I love to write and reflect a lot on what makes me tick, I set aside time to journal almost every day of my solo missions. I highly recommend that every solo traveler purchase a journal and carve some time out to record what they are thinking and feeling along the way. It is therapeutic, and tends to calm the loneliness you may feel because the feelings are getting out and being put on paper.

Every solo trip also deserves a day of rest and relaxation. Absolutely meet new people, try new things and stretch yourself, but also don't be afraid to turn down invitations from other travelers or locals you might meet and vibe with. Spend a day in bed with room service and Netflix catching up on that much needed rest, or by the pool with a cocktail doing absolutely nothing. I've found that when I feel a desire to get around others, I tend to get poolside, so I can be with people without technically having to engage, while soaking in the sun or dipping in the pool. Schedule a spa day at the hotel or a local parlor. Pamper yourself some by getting a manicure, pedicure, or massage. These are all safe ways to be around others as a woman traveling alone. Everyone needs that once in a while.

Travel can take a lot out of you but depending on how you choose to spend your down time it can put a lot back in. The beauty of solo travel is you are on your own clock, it can contain nothing or everything. The key is following your heart and being mindful of the space you are in mentally and emotionally. Find the best balance of activities between private and social ones. As much as you enjoy the rest and relaxation moments of your solo trip you will want to be sure to strike a balance between the times of reflection and recalibration of self and being social with locals and other travelers.

Travelers new to solo adventures should section off how much time they do both. The last thing we want is for you to live in your own mind for the whole trip. Connect with locals in a structured public setting and then budget out the time that you will be fully alone. Plus, occasionally, I'll connect with someone that will lead to an actual friendship and more adventures in the following days.

My advice: Plan your time but stay open!

Packing

Tips

"*He* who would travel happily must travel light."
- Antoine de Saint-Exupery

So, you are going on vacation and it's time to pack! Are you the kind of traveler who likes to carry as little as possible or do you like to have options for the outfits you pack? Now that your trip's itinerary planning stages are complete you have a big question to respond to, 'what all should I pack?' This is your first solo adventure and depending on the type of trip you've planned you've got to be strategic. Don't let it stress you, I'll share some packing tips to make it a bit easier to start getting your things in a bag.

Let's begin with the essentials, those must have items that will be needed on every trip you go on, no matter the destination. This list isn't exhaustive, but it is what I use as a checklist for myself when I am preparing to go off into the world.

- *Passport and Travel Documents* – If you are traveling internationally your passport must be in your possession. For you to enter and exit any country you will have to show it at the airport to customs officers. My passport is quite possibly my favorite book in the world. On its pages it holds the stamps I've collected over years of group travel and solo missions. May sound dramatic, but many travelers feel the same affinity for their passports, it is truly the story of my life. I am always mindful of where my passport is on trips, and it literally can get you into most places in the world. I tend to pack my passport into my crossbody shoulder bag, that will be in my possession most of the trip. Once you've selected flights, check to make sure you have what you need to get the necessary visa for the country you are traveling to. Your passport will be checked for any required visa to enter and spend time in the country of your choosing. Visas can be cheap, for example the $25 visa upon entry into Egypt, or costly like the $163 visa required prior to entry into Ghana. Because visa costs vary, it is important to find out at the beginning of planning to factor them into your travel budget. Go on the consular website of the country you've selected to check on documentation requirements and handle those beforehand if a visa can't be acquired on arrival. You can also go onto VisaHQ.com. As of January 2019, Americans can enter 185 countries and territories without a travel visa or with a visa on arrival, so be sure to check which countries require visas upon arrival and those that require us to obtain one before arriving in the country. Visas can also take some time to process depending on where you are traveling to, so once a decision is made, begin working on securing your visa if one is required. It is important to note that when applying for visas ahead of your trip the requirements may ask that you provide different forms of documentation along with your passport. The visa application, passport sized photos, the cost of the visa, letters from your employer and other documents may be requested. Just make sure you've given yourself enough time collect all necessary documents, so you aren't scrambling just before your trip. Along with your passport and visa, have copies of your passport and other important documents on you and leave a copy with family or trusted friends in case something comes up where they would need to produce it on your behalf. If your passport is lost or stolen, having extra copies will expedite things with the consulate when working to replace it within a short time frame. Take your government issued identification (such as your driver's license) as well, this can be used in lieu of a passport if you are traveling solo domestically. If you are asked to present identification on your travels, it's a good idea to pull this out first, before your passport. The airport will ask to see one or the other when you are checking in to your flight, depending upon your destination.

- *Medicines* – If you are taking any prescription medications, be sure to pack them along with your important documents like immunization card and prescription docs. Basically, anything you need to survive should be the first thing in your bag. Having documentation showing the medicine was prescribed by a physician is a great idea, as some countries like the United Arab Emirates have strict policies regarding what drugs can enter the country, even if they are prescription. Carrying this documentation can be the difference between a quick pass through customs or being held to answer questions regarding medicines you have in your possession. Better safe than sorry, we don't want anything to hold you up from getting your vacation started! Some countries, like Kenya and Ghana, will require you to take medicines to keep from getting sick. There the government requires a yellow fever shot and strongly recommends taking a course of malaria pills. I make it a habit to take a sandwich baggie with medications that may be needed whilst on vacation like Pepto-Bismol tablets, Day-Quil and NyQuil tablets, charcoal tablets (for upset stomach), bug spray and cortisone, immunity boosters (like Airborne), ibuprofen and Neosporin. I also pack Band-Aids, because you never know when you will need them!

- *Cash and Credit and/or Debit Cards* — Taking cash in the local currency for the place you are traveling to is important, as you'll be paying for food, souvenirs and other expenses that require cash transactions. Technology may not be readily available to swipe a card. I tend to exchange money at the airport, but many avid travelers wait to get money from ATMs in the country where a better exchange rate can be had. It is completely up to you. Before leaving the country, inform your bank of your travel details so they can note your travel plans on your account and you won't be flagged for a hold on your debit and credit cards when you go. The last thing you want is to try and purchase something or withdraw cash out of the bank and it be declined. The banks will freeze your account for suspicious activity if you don't inform them.

- *Electronics* — It is important to always be prepared, maybe it's the Girl Scout in me speaking. We all know how important our cell phones have become for keeping social with those back home, but they are crucial for an even more important reason when traveling as a solo Black woman. Cell phones can help keep us safe, as they keep us connected and track our every movement. If we need to reach out to anyone for assistance, our phone is the most important electronic device we have. This essential is not one that is easy to forget to pack, as these days our phones stay in our hands, but remember to put portable chargers and cords in your bags as well. When I travel, I like to have 2 portable chargers with me, because often when I leave my hotel room at the beginning of the day I don't return until the evening. Be it to charge my cellphone during a day tour of the city or charging my wireless headsets and speakers on a beach day, I rarely leave home with out them. Be sure to pack these along with any other must have electronic device, like a camera, universal travel adapter, selfie stick/monopod, or tripod.

- *The Simple Things* — In my carry-on I always carry travel size toiletries, a change of clothes, and a couple pairs of undergarments. This way if luggage is lost by the airline, I have the essential items to carry me through at least a day waiting on them to locate my bags. I highly recommend that you carry something lightweight like a jumper or dress that doesn't take up a lot of space in your carry on, because it is better to be safe than sorry. No one likes to be stuck wearing the same thing or without what they need to clean up properly for days! These items are the bare minimum of what you need to be good to go just about anywhere in the world. Whenever possible, save yourself the hassle of lugging around extra stuff: remember, you can also just buy it there.

Now that you've gotten the essentials out of the way, it's time to get your clothes into a bag so you can begin your vacation. There are two mindsets you can take when packing: 1) "Team Carry-on" as my travel friends call it, or 2) "Got to Have Options."

No one way is correct, a lot of it depends on where you are going, the type of weather you will find there, and the length of your stay. If you are crafty enough to be able to pack everything you need into carry-on baggage, I encourage it.

Packing less will make you more mobile and can save you more money because when packing more you can run the risk of paying weight charges at the airport. I encourage you to invest in a couple sets of packing cubes. These are an awesome way to keep stuff organized in your main bag, and for keeping dirty/wet clothes separate. I tend to separate my evening attire from daytime and workout clothes from lounge wear. If you like to have options when traveling, I recommend buying a baggage scale so you can check the weight of your bag prior to heading to the airport. I tend to fluctuate between the two, but the more I solo travel I try to pack with the "less is more" attitude. Doesn't mean that always works! Here are a few general guidelines I tend to stick to when packing for solo adventures.

- *Pack for Your Itinerary* – Think about the number of days you are traveling and what you've already planned on your itinerary. Nine times out of ten you've already paid for these excursions and you know you are going once you reach your destination. This takes the guessing out of what you are going to need to pack for some of the days. I pack specific outfits for what I will be doing, one for every day. A good idea is to choose a base color like black, brown or navy and a contrasting color like white or beige and a color or two to accessorize and pull it all together. Keeps things simple and the accessory color can "dress up" the outfit if needed. Lightweight chinos, linen pants or skirts are my go-to items, as they are comfortable, easy to mix and match and can be dressed up or down depending on your itinerary.

If there are adventurous activities planned (I always have at least one day where I am going to do something physical like hiking, hang gliding, zip lining or white-water rafting), I plan outfits specific to those activities. I always pack a few outfits to workout in and my trainers because goals don't take a vacation just because you do.

Swim gear is a must! On every trip I've taken I always factor a day by some water into the itinerary. I have to find my way to the pool or beach. I pack 2 swimsuits, usually a bikini and a one piece for every vacation. Don't forget the other items that will make beach days easy, like a small beach bag, flip flops, a cover up, sunscreen, a book, and sunglasses.

Because everyone loves a good list, don't be afraid to write each days' outfits out. This will help keep you from overpacking. You'll be able to visually 'see' what you expect to wear instead of packing two or three tops or bottoms for the same day. Be sure to pack an outfit for daytime and nighttime, if you'll have plans in the evening. When I traveled to Bali solo in 2018, I posted in my travel groups the dates that I would be there, and it just so happened that 3 ladies from one of my Black travel groups were going to be there at the same time. We met up for dinner and drinks. You never know what you'll get in to, so always pack a couple of nice outfits that can transition from day to night (to save space) or pack 2 outfits per day. It's always good to pack for mixing and matching, so one item of clothing can cover more than a day.

Two things to remember when packing is: you are going to experience new cultures in other parts of the world, and you are a woman traveling alone. These facts should impact how and what you pack. I recommend that you pack clothes that are somewhat conservative. Many of my solo destinations took me to temples and places that are considered special and holy to the people there. Bali, Istanbul, Bangkok, Barcelona, the list goes on of cities where I had to cover my legs or shoulders when entering some of their most sacred must-see monuments and places of worship. Most temples, mosques and some cathedrals expect some level of coverage, so dressing conservatively is a great way to go if you plan to explore. I tend to take a couple of colorful pashminas or sarongs and cover my shoulders and arms if I'm wearing a tank top and it's too hot where I am to wear long sleeves all day. This lesson didn't take me long to learn because I live in Abu Dhabi and there is an expectation of dressing conservatively in respect for local customs and traditions, especially when entering places of worship. What I've discovered about myself is that I enjoy traveling solo to places like Sri Lanka, Istanbul, Bali, and Thailand that require a level of modesty in dress for women when going to important sites. It may seem unfair that there is a stricter dress code for women (no exposed legs or shoulders, etc.), but if you've chosen to travel there you should dress the part. Loose clothing in hotter places helps to keep you cool (trust me I live in the desert!), so pack some loose pants and tops, and try to stay comfortable. Jeans are designed to hold heat, so if you do go somewhere hot, pack more linen and breathable fabrics. Don't let the call for conservative dress concern you, in some places it's OK to dress more western a majority of the time, unless you are visiting a temple, mosque, or church. Familiarize yourself with traditions like this before you leave and if you aren't sure, check with a local or someone who has more experience with the place. The second point is an issue of personal safety. You are always more vulnerable when you're off your home turf and alone so compensate by dressing conservatively.

- *Full outfit items* - When packing it's important to pack for comfort, but also practicality. I think of what I can pack that will take up the least amount of space in my bag but can count as an outfit for a whole day. For example, when I travel some place warm (which is a large percentage of the trips I've taken in recent years), I've found myself packing more comfortable sun dresses, rompers, and jumpers, because they take up less room in the bag and qualifies as an entire outfit in one piece. If you transition into an early evening dinner because you won't make it back to your hotel in time, a nice sun dress will do wonders! I always pack something for my arms, like a light jean jacket or printed pashmina wrap, which can dress the sun dress up even more and keep the evening cool air or air conditioning in buildings from making you cold. I'm often told when packing, lay out everything you think you will need for your vacation, and then take half of it. Sounds a bit crazy, because what if I'll need that light sweater for cool nights, or what if I'll need that pair of sandals? The reality is if you mix and match things well or take items that are entire outfit pieces, you can take the less is more approach with no problem. Those "Team Carry-on" travelers who get everything into their carry-on luggage for extended trips have this "take half" philosophy down, after many years of trial and error. The key is to get very strategic about every outfit and pack for your itinerary!

- *Comfortable walking shoes* – Not many of us go on vacation to sit around. Even the laziest of trips I've planned included walking to see important sights at some point. Be sure to pack shoes that are comfortable enough to be worn for hours at a time. Nothing will ruin a trip faster than sore feet. Women's shoes are notoriously bad for feet. I generally pack my trainers, a pair of casual tennis shoes that can be worn with a sun dress like Converse All Stars, and sandals in a neutral color that can be worn with many things. My rule is to pack one pair of heels, typically black ones that can also be worn with different outfits I may plan on wearing if I go out at night. Shoes weigh a lot when packed, so try to keep the number of pairs you bring to as few as possible to avoid additional weight charges at the airport. This means packing shoes that are diverse in what they can be worn with. Of course, the type of shoes you pack will vary depending on your solo destination and I suggest choosing comfort over fashion, but the 'take as few as possible' rule still applies.

- *Instagram Worthy Shots* – Just because you are on a solo mission doesn't mean that you can't have a mini photo shoot in a fabulous location on your trip. We all love the beautiful travel photography we see on social media in colorful outfits around the globe. Remember that being on your own doesn't mean you are alone. If you've hired a driver or tour guide, he may turn into your best photographer. On the trips I've taken on my own where I've hired someone, they are always willing to snap some awesome shots for me. While you must be cautious when doing so, other travelers will be helpful and do the same if you ask, as you will be asked to do so for others when traveling as well. If you really want to have a professional photo experience, you can look in to hiring a photographer that is based in the location you choose to snap some great shots. Going solo means getting creative! When packing, I factor in the mini photo shoot opportunities I want to have, so I always pack 1 or 2 outfits that I know will aid in creating beautiful pictures; typically, colorful dresses, pantsuits or jumpers with patterns.

- *Diary* - I'm big on collecting and recording moments. They add up to amazing memoirs you can read when you need a reminder of a dope day in the life or want to share them with your special people. Oscar Wilde said, "I never travel without my diary. One should always have something sensational to read on the train." In other words, the story of our lives should be something amazing, and taking a solo adventure to an awesome place is tantamount to that. I encourage you to take your writing journal with you (if you don't have one then get one!) and chronicle your steps through your solo mission. It will be therapeutic during those still moments and cool to read well after you return home. Remember this fun fact, you are about to do something for the first time. When was the last time you could say you did that? Write it down!

There are some general travel items that I encourage you to pack if it suits where you are going. Select a great travel bag or suitcase, typically in a bright color so it can be easily identifiable at the airport baggage claim. Also invest in a good carry-on bag like a backpack or duffel bag. Many airlines restrict the weight that your carry-on can be, so try to not over pack your backpack. These bags will serve you well when you get to your destination and begin your itinerary. There's nothing like a reliable backpack or small travel bag to pack your daily necessities in when venturing out on your own to explore and sight see. If you're one who must carry a purse, I recommend a cross body bag, one that isn't easy stolen when you're exploring your destination. Choose your purse wisely! Fanny-packs are also a good option and come in fashionable prints and colors now. They can be worn across the body as well.

When you buy your backpack, check to see if you can lock it. Buy combination locks, so you don't run the risk of losing your key. Since it is critical that you protect your items for peace of mind, grab a couple of small, TSA-compliant combination locks (available at Wal-Mart, Target, or any local store). These are great for securing the zippers of your backpack's main compartment (because pickpockets are everywhere) and your luggage on the flight, train or bus to your destination. I tend to follow this rule of thumb regarding my bags: if you can't see your bag, it needs to be locked. Remember that your passport is your key into and out of many places, don't trust leaving it in your backpack, carry it on you even when your bags are stowed. Many have learned this the hard way: you can get along while traveling without many things but keep your money and passport close! As you navigate through countries on different modes of transportation it is something you should always remember to do. And again, be sure to get some form of travel insurance to protect yourself and your personal things that are expensive. Before leaving, make sure it is valid in the places you are visiting.

I've traveled many places solo and I realize that most of them were warm weather spots, but I am not afraid to travel to colder places too. For example, one of my favorite solo missions was to Budapest in October, and it was a bit on the cold side so fall clothes came in handy. Amsterdam is one of my favorite cities, but it rarely gets warm and even in the summer there is a chill in the air. If you select a destination that is cold, be sure to pack cold weather and rain gear. The trick to packing this kind of clothes is layering.

You may choose to bring your laptop, iPad, or other tablet to stay connected with work or socially. I tend to leave these items behind when I go on my solo missions, because when the laptop is there it's tempting to check emails or connect with work colleagues instead of enjoying the vacation. If you must, I suggest bringing the iPad or tablet, as it is smaller and can do much of the same things as the laptop but won't add a lot more weight to what you're bringing. I do like to stream some of my favorite shows to watch on vacation, so these items do come in handy. Most hotels have HDMI ports where your laptop can connect to the television to view there. Just remember that anything you can do on your laptop you can do on your tablet or smartphone. The same argument can be made for travel cameras. Nowadays the cameras on our smartphones can take the most amazing pictures, and you can immediately edit them and send them across the globe. Listen to my advice, leave as many of the electronics at home as possible, get out of your hotel room and enjoy the solo mission you've created for yourself! You won't regret it.

Plug in

or

Log Out?

"*My* alone feels so good, I'll only have you if you're sweeter

than my solitude." -Warsan Shire

Staying connected in this day and age of smart phones and social media is easier than ever before. At the drop of a hat we're able to communicate with friends and family on the other side of the world, get answers to our questions about travel where we are, look up information that will help us navigate through our vacation seamlessly, and post dope pictures from our travels abroad. Even more importantly than all that is the issue of personal safety and the impact having a smartphone has on ensuring that if needed, your approximate location can be tracked down.

There are perks to this constant connection we have with technology as it literally makes the world smaller. I suggest giving yourself limits to the amount of connection to the outside world you want to have, depending on your destination and overall purpose for your trip. Getting off the grid is liberating, and definitely something every woman should try at least once. But just because you're on a soul-searching adventure, or disconnecting from social media, does not mean that you should disappear. When I know the solo mission is calling for relaxation and an escape from the norm, I watch my airtime. When you are traveling, try to limit social media and overall technology use to a set number of hours a day and get to pampering yourself or going out to experience your location. When the purpose is relaxation, I tend to hit the beach, lounge by the pool, or go for a hot stone massage so I'm less on my phone or tablet. This isn't to say I'm totally disconnected on my trip, just practicing some restraint based on my purpose. I like to post on my solo trips because it alerts others to my safety, and it allows me to share highlights from my trip with my loved ones so they can experience it with me. I've found that this is especially important to my mom, because even though I'm 44, she still wants to know where I am and what I am doing. It reminds me that my adventures aren't mine alone!

There are times where I will go on excursions like cooking classes, photo walks, to museums and other must-see locations around the city and just take in those experiences without stopping to post on social media about them. I tell myself before leaving the hotel that the day will be spent in the moment, without distraction. During these moments I may take some pictures, but I don't post them until I am back in the hotel room getting ready to shut down for the day. At that time, I reflect on my day, journal the experiences had, and post a pic or two for family and friends to get a taste of the day's events.

To be completely transparent, there are some solo missions that I've gone to where I stayed on my social media platforms the entire time. Be it the excitement of actually making it to a bucket list location like one of the Seven Wonders of the World in the Lost City of Petra or doing something so incredibly cool like hang gliding or learning how to salsa dance in Brazil, I wanted to share those moments with my people back home. There's nothing wrong with this, and oftentimes your friends and family want to see what you're doing in real time. Whatever direction you decide to take regarding being tapped into technology will be the best one for you at that time, but don't be afraid to disconnect and be completely present in the moments that you are creating while away.

Solo missions help you to get in touch with yourself and a lot of times when we are checking emails, working on our laptops and even snapping pictures, we miss out on the moments that make the trip so special. Put the technology down and enjoy some quality time with you. At least a few times throughout the year I get the overwhelming desire to fast from technology altogether, to stop getting on social media, lay off the internet searching and silence the emails. If you can relate to feeling this way from time to time your solo mission is the perfect time to do so.

Being connected with technology goes beyond social media. There are some Apps that are crucial for solo travelers to enjoy a great experience, even if they limit their social media time on Facebook, Instagram and Twitter. The following apps are what I've found to help me through my solo adventures.

- *WhatsApp* is a great way to stay connected to family and friends when you travel alone. It is an app that operates much like text messaging, you can send media like videos and pictures in real time, voice notes and standard messages in text. I've created groups so I can communicate with multiple people at the same time through a common thread. When considering safety as a woman solo traveler this app is key. You can drop your live location to your family and friends, and it allows the lines of communication to remain open throughout your time away. It has a great video calling feature as well, for those times when you're feeling lonely or just want to see a familiar face. This app allows you to provide a status update to groups of people and is very user friendly. WhatsApp can be used anywhere in the world where there is data.

- *VPN* is a very wise investment to have. It is a virtual private network and it allows you to securely use public Wi-Fi. This is important because if you are abroad and utilize your personal credit card over public Wi-Fi your information can be accessible to others. A VPN will secure the connection, so no one has access to your personal details. In some countries public Wi-Fi is monitored, and a VPN with a US IP address will allow you to privately access the internet. VPNs can be downloaded to your phone, tablet, and laptop computer. I use StrongVPN and it is around $5 a month. If you have a VPN you can also access entertainment accounts, like Netflix (another app I can't travel without), that may be blocked or unavailable in that country. If I'm traveling for a while, I usually end up spending some time watching Netflix on public Wi-Fi and if I'm out of the country I turn on my VPN to get it to work properly. Remember that as a solo traveler you may want some down time where you can catch up on your shows, so be sure to download a VPN for easy access to them all.

- *Travel apps* like Booking.com, Hotels.com, Cheapo Air, Expedia, and airline apps are on my phone in case I need to make last minute changes to my travel itinerary. When I traveled to Sri Lanka I got to a point in my itinerary where I was tired of the city and wanted to travel to another part of the country where I could enjoy the beautiful beaches I'd heard so much about. I didn't have anything booked, so I used Booking.com to secure a hotel room and got my driver to take me there. Last minute bookings will happen from time to time for the solo traveler, because you can do that, there's no one traveling with you to stop you! Keep these apps on your phone in a "Travel" folder for easy access.

- I utilize *Google Maps* a lot to navigate by car in my everyday life. It offers maps for driving, public transit, and walking which makes it ideal for getting around an unfamiliar city when traveling solo. You can download maps of your destination before leaving home to use offline. I like to use Google Maps when I'm in taxis so I can make sure the driver is not trying to drive me off the fastest route for an increase in fare. It adds to my comfort level when considering safety when I'm alone. Having an idea of your location is always a good thing and it makes getting around easy in any new destination. Google Maps has a cool, voice-command option that is great for solo travelers on a road trip. The only downside to Google maps is that it is heavy on data use, but you can use it offline once you have the map saved.

- *Google Translate* is a great app to have because it makes communication easier with locals and when trying to decipher and navigate through the city where you are. Using your phone's camera, you can translate street signs and with the microphone you can talk to someone in their language. Google Translate has been very helpful for those times I've traveled alone and hadn't hired a local guide to help translate information for me. This app's many purposes come in so handy! Simple step-by-step instructions will guide you through every application. I truly don't travel without it anymore.

- Because I love to eat well when I'm on vacation and I like to plan ahead I love the Open Table app. This app lets you find restaurants based on location, popularity, price, and availability. As a woman traveling solo, you don't always want to use the hit or miss method, where you wander into a restaurant you come across and hope the food is good. I like to read reviews, look at the location of the restaurant in relation to my hotel, take a look at the food options, and book seating ahead of time if necessary. You can read restaurant reviews, see menus, learn the costs, and make reservations on the fly.

- Weather can often be the difference between a great or awful travel experience. It can even get you to change travel plans from one destination to another to avoid it. Sometimes you've already got everything booked and move full steam ahead with the vacation. For this reason, I suggest making use of a weather app on your phone, that tracks what the weather is ahead of your trip so at least you can plan accordingly. When I went to Thailand, I was prepared for the spotty rain showers that popped up because I'd researched not only the typical weather for the area but the actual weather that I would experience on my trip there. I had a poncho and umbrella packed and ready. Start checking the weather before you leave home every morning leading up to your trip for updates. I continue to check it when I arrive to my destination so I know if I'll need sunscreen or an umbrella and can dress for it. This will save you from wasting time while on your solo vacation trying to find items there that can protect you from the weather.

- When I traveled to Ghana I decided to connect with that experience more by downloading the Audible app and getting access to a free Audio book about Ghana. I selected 'Homegoing' by Yaa Gyasi, which I listened to and made connections between what I was seeing in Ghana and what I was hearing in the book. It made the experience even more powerful than it already was. I strongly encourage you to download an audiobook through Audible if you love to read but don't have as much time as you'd like to do so. It's a great app to have as you travel solo, because they are great for road trips, long flights, or just sitting and relaxing by the pool or on the beach. Your phone and a pair of headsets are all you need.

Just Be. . .

"*Traveling has taught me a lot about life, other people, and myself. It has given me some of the greatest gifts imaginable.*"
- *Anonymous*

*L*ook at solo travel as this journey that you are setting off on. Many people focus on getting to the destination rather than enjoying all that the journey has to offer. Sometimes your solo mission will include detours--those unexpected moments where the itinerary you've constructed in your head doesn't match what's happening in real time.

This happened to me when I went to Italy in 2017. Starting in Venice, I planned to head by train to Milan before leaving by plane to Paris. While in Venice I started a great conversation with a local gentleman at a small café near the Doges Palace. I enjoy moments like these, where I meet someone local and can get a genuine feel of the location through them. You will find that if you are open to meeting new people, this will happen often on your solo missions. Whenever I meet someone new, I ask them what they recommend I see or experience before leaving the city or country. He suggested I take a train to Verona, Italy, a city between Venice and Milan where one of the first colosseums was ever built and the location Shakespeare wrote about in Romeo and Juliet (where you can visit the balcony where Juliet called out to Romeo) is located.

During that conversation I made the decision to buy a train ticket to Verona and see these things for myself. That's the beauty of solo travel, you can do exactly what you want to do, there is no need to get consensus from the group on your next steps. I sent out a message to other black travelers in my travel groups online and asked if anyone would be in Italy on the dates I was, and if anyone wanted to meet me in Verona for sightseeing and a meal. I was in luck because I met up with another Black woman traveling solo who was open to passing through Verona as well. We had a great time exploring that beautiful city and made a connection that we still hold today through travel. These spur of the moment decisions that happen when you're traveling alone can lead to some amazing experiences. The key is to recognize when you can and should step away from your planned itinerary and go off the beaten path. I mentioned this story because I have always been a planner, I like to have things very organized and know what my next steps are before leaving out into the world, but through solo travel I've uncovered a piece of myself that is willing to "go with the flow" more--to loosen up and allow myself to do something outside of my norm. That is a freedom you will find as well. It's all about discovering yourself. It's more about the journey than the destination.

Growing up in a family of five you get used to the road trips as a large family unit, I rarely experienced trips without the family or at least one other person. We have always had a case of wanderlust, which led my sisters to both become flight attendants. My first trip abroad was to Paris when I was 22 years old and it was the most amazing experience for me. I realized that the world is much smaller than we were taught to believe, and that everything is accessible to us. I was so impressed by the feeling I had abroad that I began to look for teaching positions in Europe but was too afraid to leave the comfort of my family unit. Wow have things changed! My point here is, this journey of travel that I've been on started with a family focus and ultimately has grown to a reliance on self. I no longer fear stepping out and handling things outside of my comfort zone on my own. Solo travel does that for you.

To be honest, all my solo travel has been abroad, and when I'm in the United States, I rarely think of traveling by myself. I'm not sure if it's because I'm from there, and the thought of solo travel domestically doesn't feel like I've really "gone" anywhere or what. These are silly thoughts, but the exciting thing about the US is that every state carries its own traditions, from foods to speech patterns and history--almost like countries abroad do. You can literally go from one state to the next and feel like you've entered another country because they can be so different. I look forward to exploring my own country solo and encourage you not to rule the States out yourself. As I think about the relationship I've had with travel growing up in a big family, it's no wonder I never thought of going on a trip on my own. What I've learned is that you don't need a travel partner to take a memorable vacation. Traveling solo can be a rich and rewarding experience. If you allow it to be, it can be an opportunity to learn about yourself as well as about your destination in different ways. It is a good way to push yourself out of your comfort zone, forcing you to interact with others, test your bravery, and build confidence along the way.

Solo Travel is Lifelong Learning

I'm always looking for ways to continually grow and evolve as a person. With each new solo traveling experience I discover new things about myself, am challenged, gain self-confidence and independence, and learn about the world around me. It's so easy to get comfortable with the lives we've created, that we look up and years have gone by with few tales to share. You've decided to step out and complete a solo mission because you too are ready to stretch yourself and challenge your limits. I hope that the ideas and tips shared in this Solo Travel guide help to make this adventure one that lends itself to great storytelling for years to come, but the things you learn about yourself and the world are even more important things than those. Solo travel has not only taught me things, but it's given me things as well.

Since I began traveling on my own 5 years ago, I've been exposed to other cultures, put into unfamiliar situations that required spur of the moment decisions, and at times put into emotional, stressful, and difficult situations. Don't let that statement scare you, everything that happens on the road, good or bad, teaches you something and helps to build new skills. I'd dare to say that these skills learned have prepared me for life. Don't get me wrong, you will always learn a lot no matter how you travel, as a couple or with a group, but it is intensified when you are traveling alone.

On my first solo trip it became increasingly clear early on that I was going to sink or swim on my own. I had no one there to hold my hand and get me through tough situations or to help me make decisions. It was all on me. That fact builds an independence that relying on only yourself brings. There's no group to help you navigate a city or solve problems that pop up because it's just you. Solo travel is a great thing because as you gain the strength and confidence that comes with handling things you gain useful skills for life. I'm going to share the things solo travel has taught and given me, and I hope that after you travel alone more your list greatly exceeds mine.

Solo Travel Skills

- *Budgeting Skills* - One of the most important things traveling solo has taught me is how to budget better. Before I began traveling solo, I participated in group trips where major costs were split, and I could be a little less focused on my spending. Once I began traveling on my own dime, I had to learn how to make my money last while still enjoying an awesome itinerary. It forces you to be more disciplined in your pre-trip spending and to be creative in your itinerary planning. Every trip requires some budgeting skills and there is a trick to making money last. The more you travel solo the easier it gets to plan, budget, and become strategic with your spending so you can splurge some or pick up what you want to bring home. Planning your travel budget well and making wise decisions gets easier with time. I'm thankful because this skill has helped me budget more in my everyday life, most likely because I'm always saving for my next trip!

- *Communication Skills* – When you travel you learn how to communicate in many ways with the world around you. On my solo trips the fact that non-verbal language speaks volumes has become even more clear. No matter where I roam, I am conscious of my body language when interacting with others. My overall communication skills have gotten better since I began solo travel in recent years. You learn how to communicate with people when you are traveling alone, especially when those around you may speak a different language. I have to say that my language skills have improved as a result as well. As a solo traveler in a country that doesn't speak your language, you'll quickly pick up on basic words and phrases. The more you speak with people, the more you'll start to understand their language. I've grown more patient with others when we are trying to understand each other, and this skill has bled into my everyday life. Communication is key! Traveling alone doesn't exempt you from interacting with others no matter how much you plan to stay to yourself. You'll have to make sure you order your food correctly, haggle with people in the markets, speak to customer service reps at hotels, and you'll be socializing with other travelers and locals. It takes both verbal and non-verbal communication to get through a trip smoothly. I've found that wearing a smile is a little thing that brings people to you. Since non-verbal body language is the loudest form of communication, an initial smile when engaging with someone can make them want to show you the best of their country and culture, show you around and be happy to assist in any way. Never underestimate the strength of your body language when traveling solo, it can make a world of difference.

- *Navigation Skills* - We all have our comfort zones. For most of us, the city we grew up in or currently reside make up these boundaries because we can easily get around. Traveling alone requires you to get around a new city or country independently. If you are unsure of yourself don't be afraid to ask for help. Most cities have welcome centers near areas of transit or in central areas downtown. Don't stand around looking confused because that will not get you where you want to go, and you'll end up really looking like a tourist. Be prepared to read a map if you're going to get anywhere and can't be helped. When I was planning my "Tour of Italy," I planned my route before I left the States because I was crossing the country by train with stops in different cities. Whether you're just trying to get from your hotel to a must-see attraction on the other side of town or you're planning your route to the other side of the country, your navigational skills will have no choice but to improve quickly. After you've applied these skills in a foreign country alone you will return home a map master. The initial fear of unfamiliarity with the location will dissipate after the second or third day of navigating your location. By the second or third solo trip number you'll feel like a human compass. Get out there and get lost, you'll find your way back every time!

- *Problem Solving Skills* – Let's face it, no matter how much planning you put into your solo mission there are bound to be some hiccups. The thing about it is you are the only person who can solve them when you're traveling by yourself. You learn how to be a problem solver quickly because of this. A lot of problems can arise while traveling from the airline losing your luggage, breaking or losing your phone, something being stolen from your bags, or the accommodation you booked "lost" your reservation. You can and will solve them! Some things will be outside of your control and some may be your fault, but the bottom line is you will have to figure them out all on your own. Add on the fact that you won't be on your home turf but in a foreign country, so your skills will be sharpened quickly. The more you do it, the better you become at solving issues. Problem solving is a skill that transfers to every area of life, so well after your solo trip ends these will serve you in life. I've found that finding answers and little bumps in the road don't faze me anymore and I'm grateful to my travel experiences for this.

- *Decision Making Skills* – My family traveled a lot together and having two sisters in the travel industry made it easy for the rest of us to sit back and allow them to take the lead with planning, navigating cities and making big decisions regarding the family trips we were taking. Once I moved abroad and started traveling on my own, I began taking these responsibilities on for myself. As a solo traveler, there's no one else there to hold your hand or walk you through making decisions regarding your trips. Every decision is all up to you--where to stay, which attractions to visit, your travel route, what tours to partake in, how long you'll stay in any one place, every decision, big or small is yours. When problems arise, you'll find yourself making quick decisions as well. Such an important life skill to master. As I reflect on my solo missions it amazes me how many decisions are made in a day, and this will become much easier to do at home too.

As I've noted throughout this guide one of the best parts of taking solo missions is the growth that comes from every experience. When I talk to people about my travel experiences, they ask me about the expenses of the trips and I always remind them that "experiences are currency." What you get from your journeys far exceed what you've spent to get there.

One of the best parts about solo travel, in my opinion, is how much you can learn and grow during that experience. Now I can't say that everyone grows and becomes a more centered and deeper person just because they are traveling, but it is a great opportunity to see what you are made of, challenge your limits, and step outside of your comfort zone in many areas of your life.

How can these things not lead to some type of change, big or small? It's not that everyone changes and becomes a different person just because they're traveling solo, but it's a good opportunity to push yourself. Traveling alone can really teach you a lot about life and how to navigate its many obstacles, especially if you are open to personal growth. I know that I've applied the skills I've learned while traveling alone into my everyday life and I feel I am a better version of myself because of it.

I've shared what solo travel has taught me, now let me get a little deeper into what it has given me.

- *Deeper Levels of Independence* – I've always considered myself to be an independent woman. I'm used to taking care of myself, setting goals and getting things done. As one who enjoys my own company, I have never minded doing things on my own. Solo travel has built a deeper understanding of what makes me tick, I've learned more about who I am and exactly what I'm capable of when I step out into the world and "get lost." Solo missions will teach you true independence, that ability to take care of yourself, which goes deeper than just enjoying being alone. When you're out there, you can't neglect yourself, your finances, your health, and all the things that come with being an adult outside of their comfort zone. I'm excited that you are taking this solo trip, because if you aren't already an independent person you will be on the road to become one. You may find that you enjoy taking care of everything yourself.

- *Confidence* – It's amazing what setting off into the world can do for your confidence! You will feel an abundance of self-confidence when you're in the midst of that first solo excursion into the world, things are flowing right on the itinerary you've created, you're handling issues that arise like a boss, and it hits you that YOU DID THAT! You are here, in a space that you constructed for yourself, away from the safety net of home, around unfamiliar people and surroundings and yet you're thriving. Your confidence can't help but be boosted. You will find that you second guess yourself less and less, you stand firm in your decisions and aren't afraid to stand up for what you believe in. Having a high level of confidence as Black Woman in this world is critical. I love the feeling that proving to myself that I have no limits gives. As you continue to travel solo, you'll see what you are capable of and this confidence will continue to grow.

• *Positivity* – Some people always see the cup half-full. People around me tell me that I am a positive and happy person and I am glad that the vibes they are feeling from me are good. But let's be realistic, not everyone is positive and happy 100% of the time. We all have those days where the mood is heavy and it can be hard to lift it. I can say that since I began traveling solo my level of joy and sheer happiness has multiplied ten-fold. I have many more joyful days than moody ones and I account a lot of that to my solo missions. When I feel the need to recalibrate, recharge, and reboot because the pressures of the world or life begin to weigh me down, I begin planning a solo trip with one purpose in mind: getting re-centered. Don't get me wrong, you don't want to have to "get away" every time you are feeling some kind of way, but what solo travel does is allow you to reconnect with that calming part of yourself that helps you to get focused on what your blessings are versus the negative thoughts that pop up. If I can't travel far, I may do a staycation at a nice hotel, where I spend my weekend at the spa, on the beach, or eating room service in a plush robe watching Netflix. Solo travel quiets the world and allows us to be with ourselves. As Black Women we hold so many things down from work to family, and I'm thankful for the opportunities to just be in the present with myself. These moments lead to a more positive person on the other side.

- *Trust* – Being a woman traveling alone you must be careful who you allow yourself to trust just for most basic of safety reasons. We must trust our instincts and protect ourselves, which can sometimes lead to us assuming the worst about others we meet who may have the most genuine of intentions. I make it a practice to trust my gut first, to stay aware and alert, and that is tied to my personal safety and trusting that they won't steal from or hurt me. I've developed a different kind of trust through solo travel that includes being open to new people and making genuine connections with others on the road. I've learned that I don't have to be so guarded with sharing a piece of myself when I meet others that have a lot in common with. This willingness to exercise the extrovert portion of my introverted-extrovert personality leads to more enjoyable trips and being a more open person at home. Stay open to people. This is not to say to trust everyone that you meet on your solo missions but allow yourself room to trust others and ultimately yourself.

- *Freedom* - Sometimes, when you grow up in the United States you can feel detached from the rest of the world. If your family doesn't have the means to travel abroad, you may see the rest of the world as this unobtainable space--one you may have a desire to experience, but can't. Solo travel has given me the freedom to see the world, on my terms. No restraints, no rules, no one telling me how my experience should "look," just my own genuine connection with the earth. I feel freedom to move about and explore whenever I want. Going solo lets you decide every aspect of your experience, which is so freeing. When I travel alone, I have the freedom to completely be myself and to connect with others where I end up. Solo travel has allowed this Black Woman from Michigan to experience places I've only read about in books, to meet new people, and given me the freedom to live.

- *Acceptance* - Travel has given me is a stronger level of acceptance. When you grow up and see everyone existing in about the same way in your neighborhood and even in a broader sense in your country, you don't have a true understanding of how other people outside of your frame of reference are living. Through my travels I've gotten a chance to meet people from all over, to visit their homes and communities, and to see how their lives connect with my own. The biggest thing I've learned is that we aren't that different at all. Being a black person and a woman, we often aren't accepted in society despite the strengths we carry. For this reason, I've always been accepting of other people, of other cultures, of other beliefs, etc. When people say travel is the best teacher, I must agree 100%. I try to be understanding of the culture where I am and believe that we must always seek to understand the customs of the place we are visiting. Watch everything from the way the locals are dressed, to the significance of ceremonies you attend. Ask a lot of questions because there is no point going into the world if you don't want to learn about it. Oftentimes, I'll purchase clothing from local markets of what the locals are wearing along with pieces of traditional art and jewelry from my travels to share with those back home about the culture where I was.

Allow Yourself to "Get Lost"

Whenever I feel it's time to head out on another solo trip, I start to tell my family and friends that I am ready to "get lost" for a moment. They automatically know what that means; I'm about to complete a solo mission.

It's important that you recognize who your cheerleader is. Everyone has a "cheerleader," that one person who hears that you're starting to plan a solo trip and supports and encourages you the entire way. Find out who that person is for you and stay around their energy. There will be enough people spreading their anxiety and opinions about you traveling alone. You'll need to balance it out with the positive vibes this person has about you conquering your fears and taking the leap into the unknown. It's healthy to allow yourself the freedom to wander, allowing each day to take you where it will, without anyone else's input into your journey. We don't do that enough.

Try to have a healthy balance between taking each day slow and pampering yourself, participating in activities and tours, and allowing yourself to get up in the morning with no agenda and allowing the day to control the outcome. When I say "get lost" I don't mean literally, I mean go with out a plan and see where you end up. It's literally picking a direction and just walking. Maybe you wander into a café for lunch then visit an art gallery before doing some shopping or taking in a sunset river cruise. It literally means allowing yourself to experience your solo trip without a plan. Try it at least once!

There is a certain level of freedom that you will feel that will make the solo trip completely worth it. Traveling, no matter how little or how close to home you may be, really can open your eyes and teach you so much. I encourage everyone to go out on a solo adventure, and then another one and another one. When you return home after engaging with other cultures you will feel like a citizen of the world.

Being Black and A Woman in the World

I purposely waited until the end of this guide to give some insight into how solo travel impacts the Black Woman. As with most people venturing out alone, the questions of how the world will receive you rise to the surface, but no more so than I imagine they do for us. There are perceptions about Black Women in different parts of the world due to history in those areas, something that is ingrained into the fabric of the location and aren't easily released.

I remember reading an article about a Black woman traveling solo in parts of Eastern Europe and how, although she was highly educated and presented herself well, people immediately took her for a prostitute at first seeing her. These events happened again and again as she navigated this part of Europe. People were not warm and welcoming as they had been on her other solo adventures to other parts of the world. In most new cities she visited, she was solicited more times than she cared to count. Reading that, it hit me just how difficult it is to be who we are everywhere else, not just in the United States.

So why am I sharing this?

I share this story to say, that even though I haven't experienced her story myself (just some of the usual "what are you doing over here" stares), SHE IS ME, and I have to know how I would handle such situations should they arise when I travel alone. By no means am I telling you to select countries other than Eastern Europe for your solo missions. People in these places just need more exposure to understand that we are more than what they've perceived us to be.

I'm sharing this story to get you thinking about how you will approach situations that may come up when you set off on your solo missions. This entire guide has been about preparation for getting lost in the world, so I want to prepare you for this too.

Just like in the States, people will love you and hate you too. Luckily for us, we have long since found ways to deal with these attitudes, and that ability will serve us well should we need it elsewhere. I tend to take on the "nothing surprises me attitude," so I won't be thrown when something out of bounds like this happens. How you decide to respond to situations that are somewhat annoying or unsettling will determine what you get out of the trip. People's response to seeing Black people are different no matter where you go, so don't allow one bad experience to sour you to traveling solo.

For example, people in many Asian countries will make you feel like Beyoncé, even if you can't carry a note. They will come and ask to take pictures with you, and some may not even ask, they just want footage to prove you were there. They may walk up and touch your hair or get into your personal space without permission. The truth is, they aren't exposed to many Black travelers in those countries. All they know is what they get from the media, they truly mean no disrespect. In a way we are ambassadors for our race when we travel abroad, because for some we are the only Black people they may ever encounter. When I take on this perspective and remind myself that people are people, I release any negative feelings and embrace the moments. Pretty soon I'm posing for pictures with them like they are the paparazzi.

Of the places I've traveled solo, only one caused me discomfort in feeling like I wasn't welcome as a Black woman in that space, it was only a moment, and then it was gone. Remember that everyone's experiences are not your own, you just walk knowing that they happen. I've been blessed not to have issues with others when traveling solo. In fact, I've met some of the kindest and most beautiful spirits out there in places worlds away from my comfort zone. My biggest tip would to be to stay positive and don't let things that pop up throw off your vibe. Address it, or not, and keep moving. These journey moments are what build character and make us stronger.

In this guide I've shared tips that have helped me as a Black woman traveling solo when I've purposely chosen to go off on my own into the world. I've tried to bring what I've learned through my experiences to you, so you can feel inspired to step out and wander. Solo travel isn't easy. There are a lot of decisions that go into crafting an unforgettable experience before you even leave home. You'll battle the ideas of others, budgeting woes, the bouts of loneliness, concerns over safety, and even the awkwardness of that first meal or activity you do alone. All these things are okay, they are a part of the journey to discovering exactly what you are made of.

From birth, Black women have been gifted with strength, courage, perseverance, and tenacity. What solo travel does is boost these gifts to another level. When we return home after a trip, we aren't the same, we've left something where we were and picked up something new. We've discarded fears, biases, dependence, and uncertainty about ourselves in the world and picked up life skills that will carry over into our everyday lives.

Johann Wolfgang Von Goethe wrote, "Nothing can be compared to the new life that the discovery of another country provides for a thoughtful person. Although I am the same, I believe to have changed to the bones." The confidence to embark on a solo mission isn't readily found in all of us, it's built and starts with the first step off the plane. It is my hope that what I've shared from my solo missions has given you an outline for what to do to prepare, enjoy the moments, and informed you of what skills you'll be bringing back with you upon your return.

If I can leave you with one thought it would be: "you never know what you're made of until you're forced to prove it." Solo travel forces you to leave the comfort of 'you' and discover who you were meant to be.

Solo Travel goes deep. Let It.

A GUIDE TO
INTERNATIONAL
TRAVEL

DIARY OF A TRAVELING BLACK WOMAN

Travel Diary

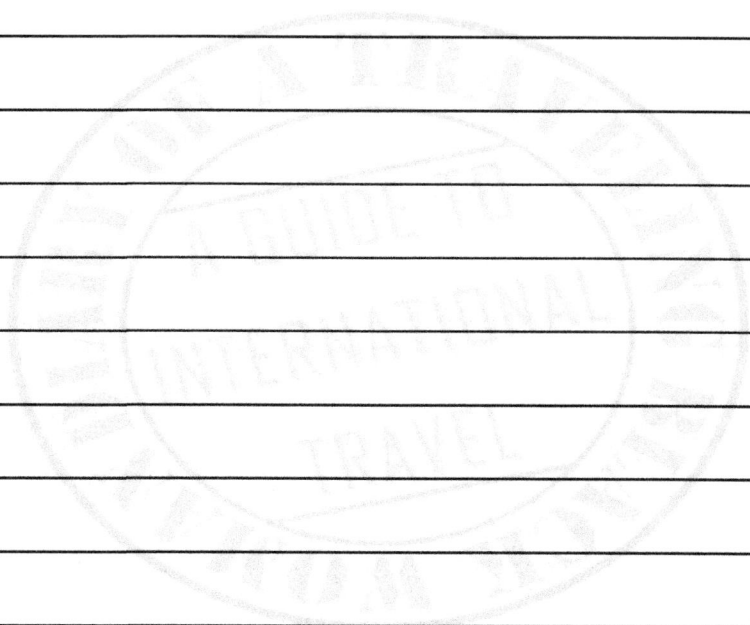

_____

_____

_____

_____

_____

_____

_____

_____

_____

_____

_____

_____

_____

_____

_____

_____

_____

_____

_____

_____

_____

About the Author

*M*arilene Shane, a native of Detroit, Michigan, is an established educator and school leader who has been living abroad in Abu Dhabi, United Arab Emirates for 5 years. She has visited 25 countries and counting, and traveled to 11 of those countries solo.

Marilene believes solo travel allows for personal growth, releases fears, and helps you to connect to the world in the most authentic way. Marilene hopes this guide will foster a love of "solo missions" in Black women around the globe.

Follow Marilene's travels on Instagram:

@wander_lene

Printed in Great Britain
by Amazon